Summoning Hull

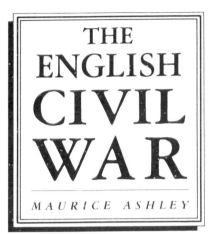

THE
ENGLISH
CIVIL
WAR

MAURICE ASHLEY

THE
ENGLISH
CIVIL
WAR

MAURICE ASHLEY

ALAN SUTTON

First published by Thames & Hudson Limited in 1974
This revised and reillustrated edition published in the United
Kingdom in 1990 by
Alan Sutton Publishing Limited · Brunswick Road · Gloucester

British Library Cataloguing in Publication Data
Ashley, Maurice, *1907–*
The English Civil War
1. English Civil War
I. Title
942.06'2

ISBN 0–86299–708–9

Jacket illustration: The surrender of the city of York to the
Roundheads *by Ernest Crofts. (Photograph: Fine Art Photographic
Library Limited)*

Typesetting and origination by
Alan Sutton Publishing Limited.
Printed in Great Britain by
Dotesios Printers Limited.

Contents

List of Illustrations

Permission to reproduce illustrations from the sources indicated is gratefully acknowledged.

Colour plates

Maps

Symbols used in maps on pages 69 and 104 are as follows:

Royalist cavalry   **Parliamentarian** cavalry

Royalist infantry   **Parliamentarian** infantry

●●●● **Royalist** dragoons   ◎◎◎◎ **Parliamentarian** dragoons

Maps of England and Scotland, showing the main battles of the civil war

Orkney Islands

Thurso

Dunrobin Castle

Corbisdale X

Outer Hebrides

X *Auldearn*

Inverness

R. Spey

Alford X

Aberdeen

X *Inverlochy*

R. Dee

S C O T L A N D

R. Tay

• Alyth
Dundee

Tippermuir X

Perth

Inveraray

Stirling
•

Inverkeithing

Dunfermline X

Firth of Forth

ATLANTIC OCEAN

Dumbarton

X *Kilsyth*

Edinburgh •

• *Dunbar*

Musselburgh

Berwick

Glasgow

R. Clyde

Coldstream

Hamilton

Firth of Clyde

Philiphaugh X

R. Tweed

X • *Dumfries*

Key

X   sites of main battles
△   houses besieged during the civil war

Preface

This is a fully revised version of a book first published by Thames and Hudson in 1974 and then well received. The present book contains many new illustrations including eight pages in colour and revised maps. I have completely rewritten the accounts of the battles of Marston Moor and Naseby embodying the results of the latest research. I have corrected one or two small errors and eliminated verbal infelicities; and the bibliographical note has been brought up to date.

I am grateful to Mr Alan Sutton for proposing this revision to me. I should also like to acknowledge my indebtedness to the many modern scholars who have specialized on the history of the civil war, in particular to the writings and activities of the late Brigadier Peter Young whose recent death is a sad loss to the study of military history of that time.

MAURICE ASHLEY
1990

CHAPTER ONE

Long-term Causes

Of all the mid-seventeenth-century revolutions in Europe the one that took place in England was the most complex and fascinating. It involved no fewer than three civil wars: the first was fought from 1642 to 1646; the second began early in 1648 and resulted in the trial by some of his own subjects of King Charles I, a traumatic event which was followed by his execution; and finally there was the premature attempt during 1649–51 by Charles's eldest surviving son to regain his father's throne with the aid of Irish Roman Catholics and Scottish Presbyterians, which collapsed completely after the destruction of his army at the battle of Worcester.

All this happened in three sparsely populated kingdoms. Though one speaks (correctly) of the English revolution and the English civil wars, one has to remember that, politically at least, two occurrences that led to the conflict in England were the vain attempt by Charles I to suppress in 1639 and 1640 risings by his Scottish subjects, compelling him after an interval of eleven years to recall an English Parliament to ask it for financial aid, and the Irish rebellion which broke out in the autumn of 1641, sparking off civil war through an unresolved argument about which side was to control the English armed forces recruited to suppress it. Thus rebellions in Scotland and Ireland gave rise to civil war in a country with a much larger population, where the members of the governing classes – 'the political nation' consisting of the monarch and his Court, the peerage and the leading landed classes – mostly knew each other and had much the same habits and spent the same kind of lives. It was the split down the middle that developed among these ruling classes which brought on the war. To begin with, at any rate, the mass of ordinary people was little affected by the row between their masters.

As a contemporary wrote, 'They care not what government they live under so as they may plough and go to market.' Another noted somewhat differently that 'there were very few of the common people that cared much for either of the causes but they would have taken any side for pay and plunder'.

Should the English revolution be attributed mainly to an economic 'crisis' in society? During the sixteenth century important economic and social changes had been taking place. The price of food doubled between 1500 and 1550; by 1590 it had almost quadrupled; and in 1640 the price of food was about six times what it had been in 1500. The causes of the price inflation were various. The influx of silver from Central and South America to Spain in effect depreciated the value of money throughout Europe; a 'population explosion' occurred, increasing demand; and lastly, in England, the sales of Church and in particular monastic property following the Protestant Reformation in the reigns of King Henry VIII and his son Edward VI created a state of economic confusion which may well have reduced agricultural output. Wages did not keep up with the increase in prices and neither did rents that had been fixed over long periods of time through leasehold agreements. Thus a state of general unrest was created among landlords, their tenants and the small cottagers or landless labourers.

But by 1590 the difficulties brought about through inflation were almost over. 'Around the 1580s the land market began to boom . . . and boomed for the next half century' (J.H. Hexter). Rents started to catch up and even run ahead of prices. Landed incomes, whether derived from rents or from direct farming, rose considerably towards the end of the sixteenth century and the early part of the seventeenth. Landlords grew more cautious about granting long leases and as soon as leases fell in heavy fines were imposed for their renewal or rents were raised. Thus landed incomes grew rapidly after 1590 and an increase in agricultural profits, especially from sheep-farming, took place. The theory that no profits were made from land by the smaller gentry in the years that preceded the outbreak of the civil wars and that the only way in which the aristocracy and the gentry could acquire real wealth was by obtaining gifts and offices from the King is no longer generally accepted. No doubt some landlords got into financial difficulties owing to extravagance or incompetence, but the

Drawings relating to prophesies made by Paulus Grebnerus in 1582. The annotations in Latin indicate that three years of plenty were predicted [under Oliver Cromwell], followed by famine from *c.* 1663. These were published by 'William Lilly, Student in Astrology' in his study *Aenigmaticall Types of the future State and Condition of ENGLAND for many years to come*, published in *Monarchy or no monarchy* (1651)

majority were better off and had gained from the boom. Nor was it only the upper classes who benefited: it is clear that the yeomen, both small freeholders and leaseholders, were also waxing richer. It has been suggested that merchants and industrialists (who formed less than 10 per cent of the community) did not enjoy the same rise in profits before the civil wars as the landed men did. But even if that were so, it was certainly not members of this class who became eager agents of rebellion. Their preference was for peace, for war merely interrupted the course of trade.

A great deal of elaborate statistical work has been done during the last forty years or more aiming to show a decline in the financial, social and political strength of the aristocracy from which the rising

This portrait of James I (1566–1625) was painted by the Dutch artist Daniel Mytens
(1590–?1648) in 1621

The great patron of the arts in the seventeenth century, Thomas Howard, 2nd Earl of
Arundel (*c.* 1585–1646), is painted here by Daniel Mytens. Arundel commanded the
King's armies against the Scots in the two so-called Bishops wars, but was renowned
more for his artistic interests than his military abilities. Clarendon wrote that he had
'nothing martial about him but his presence and his looks'. In this picture, painted
c. 1618, Arundel is shown presenting the fine collection of classical statuary in his
gallery: he was the first collector of such works in England and, having increased his
fortune by marrying the heiress of George Talbot, Earl of Shrewsbury, he became one of
the greatest collectors of his age

5

gentry and yeomanry profited. It has been stated that the sixty peerage families which existed about 1540 had been obliged to sell off much of their land. 'There is overwhelming evidence', Professor Lawrence Stone has written, 'that the holdings of the surviving peers of 1558 [that is to say the forty peers who remained when Queen Elizabeth I came to the throne] had fallen by about a quarter by 1602 and by a further fifth by 1645.' Thus the average landholding by all peers declined by nearly a half as compared with the holdings of the same peers who existed in 1558. Their real incomes had fallen correspondingly. So, it is argued, there was 'a crisis in the aristocracy' owing partly to the static rents received by the nobility during the years of the price inflation, partly to the need for them to indulge in conspicuous consumption in order to maintain their social status, and partly to incompetent management of their estates. No doubt, like the landed gentry as a whole, some peers 'fell' and some 'rose'. Yet several peerage families did exceedingly well, for example, out of sheep-farming; the Earl of Northumberland, the Earl of Devonshire, the second Earl of Salisbury, the Earl of Newcastle and the Earl of Worcester were all extremely wealthy men; so too in the first half of the seventeenth century were the Talbots, the Howards, the Spencers, the Montagus and others. An examination of the economic situation in eastern England in the Elizabethan and Jacobean periods has shown that there only the Crown and Church granted long leases. The fact is that the aristocracy, like the wealthier gentry, could 'stand a great deal of ruin'. Nor is it at all easy to distinguish between the aristocracy, the victims of this 'crisis', and the 'rising gentry' who are said to have grown in economic and political stature at its expense. Why should the younger sons or relatives of peers or the new peers created lavishly by King James I and King Charles I be differentiated from members of the ancient peerage, that is to say the peers who survived the reigns of Henry VIII and his children? Can one really isolate convincingly the economic classes that existed four hundred years ago?

The fact is that no separation between rising peers and declining peers or between rising gentry and declining gentry offers any significant explanation of the long-term causes of the civil war. Some rich men were Royalists and some thriving gentry families were loyal to the Crown. Yet a number of declining peers and gentry also sided

Charles I was artistic by nature and had extravagant tastes. The Court was treated in particular to elaborate masques, and here we see Inigo Jones's design for Queen Henrietta Maria's costume when she took the role of Chloris in Ben Jonson's masque *Chloridia*, staged on 22 February 1631

with the King against Parliament. In the poorer parts of England and Wales the gentry, for the most part, fought for Charles I. Indeed the mixed farming (unenclosed, or 'champion') areas such as Kent, Norfolk and Suffolk were extremely wealthy regions where the Parliamentarians were strongest, whereas in the mainly pastoral districts, such as Cheshire and Lancashire, the south-western shires and much of Wales, the inhabitants on the whole were loyal to the King. Thus the kingdom was better off than it had been for many years and it was not any economic crisis that led to the war. On the contrary, it was the growing prosperity of England, once inflation had come to an end, that made the gentry and lawyers who filled the House of Commons conscious of their claim to a much larger share in political power.

One important section of English society, however, did suffer from an economic or at any rate a financial crisis: that was the executive government of the kingdom, the monarchy itself. Queen Elizabeth I, despite her alleged parsimoniousness, had to sell property worth between £800,000 and £900,000, a lot of money for those days, just as Henry VIII had sold seven-eighths of the monastic lands which he appropriated, while in his son's reign most of the chantry lands were sold. James I, though pacific until towards the close of his reign, was grossly extravagant; so was Charles I, who had difficulty in raising resources to pay for his armies which he sent against the Spaniards and the French in 1626–7 and later the forces which he led against the Scots in 1639 and 1640. He also spent substantial sums on buying pictures and arranging masques to amuse his wife. Between 1603 and 1613 James is estimated to have sold land worth about £650,000, and between 1625 and 1635 Charles I disposed of property worth about the same amount. The land revenues of the Crown were estimated to have yielded less than £10,000 a year on the eve of the dissolution of Parliament in 1629. A wealthy peer or a merchant might have enjoyed a higher income from his investments than that.

The consequence was that in order to pay for foreign wars Charles I was driven to raise money by every conceivable means at his disposal. Even after peace abroad had been obtained, since he refused to allow Parliament to sit between 1629 and 1640, he levied tonnage and poundage (that is to say duties on imports and exports) without parliamentary permission and in face of much discontent among the

An Allegory of Peace and War by Rubens. The picture was presented to Charles I by the artist, who had come to London as diplomatist in 1629 to arrange a truce between England and Spain. It was described in the King's catalogue as 'an Emblin wherein the differrences & ensuences betweene peace & wars is shewed'

merchants who had to pay it, notably in the City of London. The Customs were collected by 'farmers' who paid the Government large sums of money in advance out of which they earned a handsome profit. A test case (Bate's case) in the reign of James I had conferred upon the Crown the prerogative right to introduce new impositions as supplements to the existing Customs duties. During the treasurership of Lord Portland, for example, new duties were levied upon coal and taxes on imported tobacco increased. The Exchequer judges upheld the King's right to collect the proceeds of these duties. In addition irritating feudal rights belonging to the Crown, which had fallen into disuse, were revived. Lord Portland was delighted by the idea of fining all gentlemen who owned land worth £40 or more a year if they refused to accept the dubious honour of knighthood.

This engraving of *The Soveraigne of the Seas*, which was built in 1637 and was the most powerful and, some said, the most beautiful warship yet produced for the royal navy, was published as propaganda for the revival of the Elizabethan 'ship money'

Patents, which their critics called 'monopolies', were granted, for example, for new ways of making soap and refining salt. Above all, Charles I's Government revived an Elizabethan tax known as 'ship money', which had been levied on seaports and coastal counties to pay towards the cost of the royal navy. In 1635 the tax was extended from the coastal areas of England to inland counties. It was a thoroughly economical tax, easy to collect, for the duty of doing so was given to the Justices of the Peace, who delivered the money to the sheriffs who then handed it over to the Admiralty. About £750,000 was raised by ship money during the years between 1637 and 1640 and it aroused intense indignation because everyone who

In this title-page to *Dies Dominica*, the Puritans attempted to indicate clearly suitable ways in which the Sabbath could be observed. On the left are the 'works of light' and on the right the 'works of darkness', among which the Puritans included the entertainments permitted by the reissued *Book of Sports*

had any means at all had to contribute. Although John Hampden, a wealthy Buckinghamshire squire, brought a test case over it, the judges held by a majority that the King was entitled to collect ship money if he considered that the kingdom was faced with dangers at sea (from pirates or otherwise) and that he alone was the judge of when such an emergency occurred. Thus because of his financial difficulties the King was compelled to demand money from his subjects in new and unpopular ways and it was widely considered that private property was in peril. 'What foolery is this,' remarked one gentleman, 'that the country in general shall be thus much taxed with great sums to maintain the King's titles and honours', that is to say as ruler of the Narrow Seas. So deeply was ship money disliked that in the end many people refused or evaded its payment. Just as contemporary revolts against the Spanish Government were sparked off by the imposition of new taxes, so Charles I's financial difficulties, as well as his policies, stood first among the long-term causes of the civil war.

But another long-term cause was the animosity felt towards the leaders of the Church of England by the Puritans. Some historians no longer consider it correct to write of 'the Puritan rebellion', but unquestionably the Puritans played an important part in the coming of the civil wars. The Puritans, whose beliefs about the correct procedure and organization of church services were derived largely from the French theologian, John Calvin, had been crushed during the reign of Queen Elizabeth I. But James I, who came to England from Scotland, where the Lowlands were extremely puritanical, made a serious effort to reach agreement with their spokesmen.

The Puritans thought that preaching was more important than set prayers, that an individual believer could establish a direct contact with the Almighty without the intervention of Church or priest, that he could have been elected by God to 'salvation' from the beginning of time, and that all remnants of Roman Catholic ritual must be eliminated from church services. The researches of Dr Christopher Hill have shown us many of the economic grievances felt both by the Puritans and by others against the Church of England. They resented having to pay the various tithes, that is to say taxes which might amount to one-tenth of the harvest, in order to support the Church or to meet the demands of landowners who had bought these tithes for a capital sum (these were known as 'impropriations') from the Church;

William Laud, Archbishop of Canterbury, after the portrait painted by Sir Anthony Van Dyck in *c.* 1636

they disliked the Church courts which could impose humiliating punishments on members of congregations who were deemed to have sinned; they objected to fees and dues that had to be paid by law on the occasions of christening, marriage, funerals and so on; they resented paying for the upkeep of clergy who did not preach. No doubt all that was valid, but even more significant were the sermons and exhortations of Puritan ministers or lecturers who managed to obtain access to pulpits and preached – by implication at least – in criticism of the Church hierarchy; and Charles I was after all the Supreme Governor of the Church.

Charles had in 1633 selected William Laud, who had been one of his chaplains and President of St John's College, Oxford (it was in Cambridge that the Puritan intellectuals flourished most), as Archbishop of Canterbury. Neither Laud nor his friend and patron, Richard Neile, who was to become Archbishop of York, belonged to the aristocracy. Laud was the tenth child of a Reading clothier and Neile reputedly the son of a man who made tallow candles. The austere King, who loved beautiful things and was the first Stuart to be brought up in the English Church, favoured orderly government and disliked the iconoclasm of the Puritans. Laud was no theologian but he found predestinarianism distasteful. Therefore he tried, like one of his predecessors, Archbishop Whitgift, to sweep Puritanism out of the Church. But it was too powerful and he was too late. The Puritan preachers for the most part wanted to overthrow the Church establishment and to destroy the 'tyranny' of the new archbishops: this led to a movement to undermine the political establishment as well. Convinced and comfortable in the knowledge that they were God's Chosen People, their belief in themselves intensified their ardour to reform or recondition the Church. Most bishops thought that the Puritans were politically subversive. Parliamentarians, like John Pym and John Eliot, who were critical of the Government's policies, were not basically Puritans themselves. But the Puritans became their allies. It has been suggested that some Puritans came to believe that the King would never have been obliged to recall Parliament at all if 'the Saints' had not refused to pay their taxes. At any rate it was the intransigence of the Scottish Presbyterians, who were also King Charles's subjects, that compelled him to seek the aid of two Parliaments in 1640.

This Puritan propaganda against Archbishop Laud seeks to blacken his reputation yet
further by imputing evil practices and atrocious cruelties

The theory that the first English civil war was a class war has never
been abandoned by left-wing historians. If dubious statistical arguments no longer hold water, then contemporary literary evidence is
relied upon as proof. We are reminded that the first Earl of
Clarendon, who served both Charles I and Charles II, had insisted (in
retrospect) that this was a war not about religion ('the Puritan
rebellion', it has been claimed, was 'a nineteenth-century invention')

but about property rights. Thomas Hobbes, the celebrated political philosopher, and Richard Baxter, a contemporary Puritan theologian, were both insisting that the first duty of government was to protect private property and because it failed to do so it provoked rebellion. James Harrington, another political theorist, thought the 'Gothic balance' had been upset through the acquisition of property by gentlemen, yeomen and merchants from the Church and the nobility and that the dissolution of society by such redistribution of wealth, which had begun in the reign of Elizabeth I, 'caused the war'. This analysis of a shift in the distribution of property seeks confirmation from other contemporary writers such as Thomas Wilson, who noted at the outset of the century that the gentry had improved their economic strength at the expense both of the Crown and the Church and of the smaller freeholders. An eighteenth-century historian, John Oldmixon, has even been quoted for the opinion that 'a major part of the nobility and perhaps the gentry' sided with the King in the civil war, while nine out of ten of the merchants, clothiers and middling yeomanry all along supported Parliament. But this literary evidence is far from convincing. Serious work that has been completed on county histories shows that no clear-cut picture is to be found of class conflict. In most cases the gentry was divided; as to the merchants, it was to emerge that the big trading centres were by no means unanimously for Parliament. Many in London, Bristol and Newcastle came to be committed Royalists. Furthermore it has been forcibly argued that in respect of economic interests no perceptible difference between peers, knights and gentlemen at Court and their counterparts in the country is to be discerned; thus even if a conflict did exist between Court and country it was not rooted in social and economic contradictions.

In any case is it right to job backwards from the character and economic status of the men who actually fought for and against the King when the war broke out in 1642 to the social and economic changes in an earlier period? The fact was that when Parliament was called in 1640 almost the entire House of Commons and many of the Lords were critical of the King's policies and administration, and legislation was forced through to prevent the monarchy from exploiting its prerogative rights to increase taxes. The future Earl of Clarendon himself was then among the critics of the monarchy. It is

London was one of the biggest ports in Europe. This contemporary French engraving offers useful information on the nature of the city and its people

not until the end of 1641, when almost half the members of the Commons came to the conclusion that the attack on the Crown had gone far enough, that the divisions between future Royalists and future Parliamentarians can be analysed; and an analysis that has been carried out has shown that no significant social, economic or financial differences existed between these two sides. This is not to the liking of proponents of class war, but at any rate so far as the membership of the Commons is concerned it is a fact. If any clear differences are to be discovered once the war began, they are to be found in geographical factors, as has already been suggested. But even then only a very few counties were overwhelmingly in favour of one side or the other.

One distinguished historian has insisted that the transfer of a section of the national income away from the Crown, some of the peerage and the bishops to the middle class of gentry, officials and

Charles I and Henrietta Maria with their eldest child, the future Charles II, who was born in 1630. The picture, painted probably in 1632 by the visiting Dutch artist Hendrick Gerritszoon Pot, celebrates their marriage as the union of war and peace; sprigs of olive and laurel symbolize the peace-making activities of James I and the military exploits of the Queen's father, Henry IV of France

lawyers in the sixteenth century caused a shift in 'the social balance' which helps to explain the civil war 'in depth'. Three long-term causes of the civil war are therefore to be found: a decline in the respect for the monarchy, the inability of the Church to comprehend the Puritans, and the 'crisis' in the affairs of the aristocracy. Another historian has bluntly written of 'the rise of the solid middle class of lesser landowning gentry on the ruins of the ancient aristocracy'.

Thus the 'bourgeoisie', beloved of the Marxists, are let in, as it were, by the back door. The assertion is made that to ignore the 'pre-conditions' that cause revolutions to be possible is foolish and it has been claimed that 'the view that there must be a direct relationship between social structure and political institutions . . . is widely accepted today'.

No one will deny that members of the House of Commons in the reign of Elizabeth I, James I and Charles I were more influential and more critical of the Government than they had been under the early

A Puritan satire of 1642 shows 'Rattle-Head', compounded of Laud and the Queen's Jesuit confessor, rejecting a book offered by the Puritan, 'Sound-Head', and turning instead to the monk – the true 'Round-Head', according to the Puritans

Tudors. But no member of the Commons in 1640 thought in terms of overthrowing the monarchy or even of reducing its rights, but merely of reforming it by persuading it to assuage grievances caused by a revival of feudalism. Even to assert that loyalty to the Crown had diminished is doubtful since the revolutionaries were to claim that they were fighting for the King as well as Parliament. The conclusion is that if war followed, it came about accidentally and by surprise. The genesis of the revolution is therefore not to be discerned in any class struggle, not even in 'the loss of grip' by the aristocracy. The man who lost his grip was King Charles I. The long-term causes of the first English civil war were essentially political and religious – grievances over arbitrary taxation, complaints about the organization of the Church, demands for a larger role for Parliament. By the time the war broke out the nobility was divided and uncertain about its allegiance and so was the bulk of the landed gentry. On both sides idealism was to be found. Many still believed in the divine right of monarchy and thought that in the last resort the supreme duty of a subject was loyalty to the throne. On the opposite side men of stature considered that the monarchical Government had been arbitrary in its behaviour and had betrayed the Protestant Church. Therefore the King needed to be deprived of his evil counsellors and obliged to rely upon the advice of Parliament as well as requiring its approval of his Ministers and officials.

CHAPTER TWO

Immediate Causes

Whatever the long-term causes of the civil war may have amounted to, the sequence of events that immediately led to its outbreak is not difficult to depict. It began after the accession of King Charles I to the throne at the age of twenty-five in 1625. Though his homosexual father had broken down physically and mentally in the last year of his reign, in his earlier days he had shown himself to be a shrewd politician and even at the end he offered his son some wise warnings about the future. Charles, on the other hand, was reserved, lacked a sense of humour and gave the appearance of being proud and unyielding. He was in fact highly conscientious, but was lacking in self-confidence. He had the misfortune of inheriting from his father as his principal Minister George Villiers, Duke of Buckingham, a seductive favourite who, though a courageous man, was over ambitious and at times arrogant. Buckingham made himself extremely unpopular not merely through his extravagances but owing to an unrealistic foreign policy which involved England in wars against both Spain and France.

It was because of the war with Spain that the King demanded a large sum of money from the House of Commons, though he failed to specify what he wanted it for. Naturally enough he assumed that he would get what he thought was necessary since Parliament had urged that the war should be undertaken. The Commons suspiciously offered two subsidies (about £140,000 in the money of that time) and refused to allow royal officials to collect tonnage and poundage for more than one year. The leaders in the House, such as John Pym, a well-to-do landowner long haunted by the bogy of Popery, wanted specific grievances to be remedied by the King. They were convinced that favouritism was being shown by the Court to Roman Catholics,

George Villiers, 1st Duke of Buckingham (1592–1628) dismayed the artist Rubens with his 'caprice and arrogance'. Here, in the artist's oil sketch (*c.* 1625) for the ceiling of 'my Lord's Closett' at York House, London, Buckingham is portrayed being escorted heavenwards to the temple of *Virtus* by Minerva and Mercury while Envy tries to pull him down

Buckingham made many enemies because of the supreme position he held under James I and Charles I, which provoked his early death at the hands of an assassin

especially as Charles had just married a young Roman Catholic French princess, Henrietta Maria. So Charles in a huff dissolved his first Parliament without obtaining what he wanted from it.

When his second Parliament met in February 1626, in spite of the fact that Pym and other critics of the Court had been prevented from being elected (they had been appointed sheriffs, ineligible for membership of the Commons), Sir John Eliot, a Cornish squire and a former friend of the Duke of Buckingham, took over the leadership of the House, condemned the complete failure of an amphibious attack on Spain organized by Buckingham during the previous year, and attempted to impeach him on the somewhat obscure charge of breaching 'the fundamental laws of England'. The King retorted by ordering Eliot's arrest and later dissolved Parliament. In a speech to both Houses Charles had reminded his audience that it was his right alone to summon parliaments and that if they misbehaved he would not do so. Charles's inability to extract a grant of money resulted in the imposition of forced loans on landowners and the billeting of troops on civilians. Despite such expedients the King never had the resources to make war upon another nation, let alone two. The attempt led by Buckingham in person to occupy the island of Rhé near La Rochelle, where French Protestant rebels were holding out against the Government under Cardinal Richelieu, was entirely unsuccessful during the campaigning season of 1627. In the same year five knights were arrested and imprisoned for their failure to pay the forced loan, the King refusing to show any cause for his action. Thus when, in order to obtain a money vote, Charles called a third Parliament in March 1628 the Commons, filled with landed gentry, were seething with grievances against the royal Government.

The House of Commons of 1628–9, now again led by Pym and Eliot, once more refused the King supplies until its various complaints – forced loans, compulsory billeting, arbitrary imprisonment and the imposition of martial law – had been dealt with. A 'Petition of Right' embodying these grievances was drawn up with the approval of both Houses of Parliament and reluctantly accepted by the King. Not satisfied with that, the Commons also condemned the illegal collection of tonnage and poundage and again tried to impeach Buckingham. On 26 June 1628 Charles prorogued Parliament after reminding it that he owed no account of his actions except to God and that he scorned to threaten anyone but his equals.

During the adjournment Buckingham was assassinated by a fanatic, but when Parliament met again in January 1629 its mood was unaltered. In fact it was now obvious that the King's Ministers were no longer under attack but that Charles's own actions had become the implicit subject of criticisms. These criticisms were twofold: the first related to illegal taxation, the second to the religious policy pursued by the King in his capacity of Supreme

The liuely Portraiture of Iohn Felton who most Miserably Kild The right Hono:.ble GEORGE VILLEIRS Duke of Buckingham, August ỹ 23 1628.

John Felton (*c.* 1595–1628), who assassinated the Duke of Buckingham in 1628. He had served in Buckingham's campaigns against France and Spain, and had personal as well as political grievances against him.

Governor of the Church. In spite of a somewhat ambiguous statement in his prorogation speech Charles had continued to permit the levy of tonnage and poundage. As to religion, the Commons condemned 'the growth of Popery' both in England and in Scotland and the encouragement given to 'the Arminian sect', that is to say those churchmen who believed in God's universal grace and the freewill of all men to gain salvation. As has recently been stressed, by the 1620s the Church of England had been Calvinist theologically for approximately sixty years, accepting predestination, the doctrine which maintained that from the beginning of time some men are chosen to be saved and the rest are destined for damnation. However, leading bishops appointed by Charles I did not accept this terrifying dogma. When Buckingham became Chancellor of Cambridge University in 1626 predestinarian teaching had been forbidden, while at the end of 1628 the King in reissuing the Thirty-Nine Articles originally drawn up in the reign of Elizabeth I ordered that all 'curious research be lain aside'. The Thirty-Nine Articles could in fact be interpreted as both rejecting and accepting predestination, but for the most part the Elizabethan Church had accepted it. Therefore its rejection was genuinely regarded in the House of Commons as a Popish and Arminian 'innovation' poisoning the true waters of the Christian faith. The King was asked to uphold the 'orthodox doctrine' of the Church and to have the books of the innovators burnt, while the Puritans ruminated on a fresh grievance against the Church hierarchy.

It was over these two questions, the levying of tonnage and poundage and the innovations in religion, that the clash between the King and his Parliament took place in March 1629. In spite of the protest by the Commons Charles had defiantly appointed 'Arminians' to bishoprics, chaplaincies and livings in his gift. When the Speaker of the House of Commons, acting on the King's orders, tried to adjourn it, he was held down in the chair while three resolutions proposed by Sir John Eliot were unanimously passed: the first condemned religious innovations, stating that anyone who introduced them was 'a capital enemy' to the kingdom; the second asserted that anyone who advised the levying of tonnage and poundage without the approval of Parliament was a capital enemy; the third stated that any merchant who voluntarily paid these duties

Charles I presiding in the Commons before the King and Parliament began the civil
war. The engraving is surrounded by the insignia of sitting members

was 'a betrayer of the liberties of England'. The House of Commons then broke up; another one was not to meet for eleven years.

Before turning to the startling events that occurred when parliament met again in 1640 and to the reasons why the King was obliged to summon it, let us consider the political atmosphere that prevailed during the first fifteen years of Charles's reign. Recently much research has been done by American historians on the composition and character of early seventeenth-century parliaments, based largely on diaries kept by members. It is often said that the formation of an opposition to the monarchy can be traced back to the reign of Elizabeth I and that this opposition increased in the House of Commons during the 1620s. Sometimes the term 'revolutionists' is actually applied to the leaders of this opposition. Yet it is an anachronistic view. Admittedly the House of Lords was less powerful than it had been before and the right of the Commons to petition about grievances and to vote taxes had been fully established. Yet the attitude of the first three Parliaments of Charles's reign reflected not organized opposition but a general dissatisfaction with his government. The Petition of Right was passed unanimously as were also the three resolutions moved while the Speaker was held down in his chair in March 1629. Men who subsequently emerged as convinced Royalists – such as Sir John Culpeper and Sir Edward Hyde (the future Earl of Clarendon) – concurred in the disapproval of the royal administration. Though even John Pym gave lip-service to the Divine Right of Kings, respect for the monarchy was unquestionably upon the wane. Whatever faults King James I may have possessed, he never levied taxes without parliamentary consent nor did he have members of parliament arrested without showing cause. Who was this young man of twenty-five to treat his subjects with contempt? What right had he to plunge his country into the two wars incompetently managed by the Duke of Buckingham? Why should the goods of merchants be taxed and impounded without the consent of the Commons? Was the King not defying the constitution? The general attitude was not revolutionary but conservative. Men looked back with pride to the good old days of Queen Bess. They thought that they were being confronted with innovations in the State as well as in the Church.

But the political life of the kingdom was not concentrated solely in

Eikon Basilike, of which this is the frontispiece, was the most popular work of Royalist hagiography in the mid-to-late seventeenth century, and was supposedly written by Charles I

the House of Commons. It is in the counties, where the real work of government was carried on year by year at the assizes, in the magistrates' courts, at petty and quarter sessions with the aid of information given out from parish pulpits, that one can see how the discontent over the acts of the administration was growing. Naturally the character of the discontent varied somewhat from county to county; but broadly discontents were clearly felt at the local level. Take Somerset, for example, which has recently been subjected to expert examination. Here local government was, as in practically all counties, in the hands of half a dozen gentry families. These gentry representing the county were antagonized by the extravagance and misgovernment of the upstart Buckingham. But the middling sort of the people, that is yeomen and tradesmen, also disliked the arbitrary taxes being imposed and the impressment and quartering of soldiers. It was among the county folk too that Puritan unrest with the Church hierarchy was strongest. Even Sir Ralph Hopton, who was later to be one of the ablest Royalist generals, was a Puritan suspicious of Popery and opposed to forced loans and the regular levying of ship money. The conclusion is that the county was united against the Court as it had never been before. In Kent too a united opposition of a conservative character to the Government's policies existed in the 1620s. The gentry families were prominent in objecting to ship money. Men like Sir Roger Twysden and Sir Edward Dering, who were cousins and were to fight each other in the county election of 1640, were later both to become Royalists, yet before the war they were critical of the autocracy of the King's servants from Buckingham to Strafford and thought that Archbishop Laud was a dangerous innovator. Here again the county gradually united between 1630 and 1640 against the 'Arminians', against ship-money levies, and in favour of the recall of Parliament. In Yorkshire the gentry resented not only ship money but having to pay for the King's abortive wars against his Scottish subjects; yet when the civil war began there were twice as many active Royalists as active Parliamentarians in the county. As a final example, Cornwall, which was to prove the most Royalist of all counties during the civil war and the last to surrender to the Parliamentarian armies, was also united in its grievances over forced loans, ship money and religious innovations. The forty-four members of parliament for Cornwall, led by Bevil Grenville, who like Edward Hyde (another Cornishman) and Hopton, was a future Royalist, formed a homogeneous party allergic to the King's arbitrary measures.

If one turns from political to purely religious complaints one can again note that no Puritan 'party' or formed opposition to the Church existed. Those extreme Puritans who were actually prepared to

separate themselves from the Church, the kind of men who sailed to
settle in North America, were comparatively few in number. So were
the avowed Presbyterians who wanted to abolish bishops and
substitute a form of government similar to that of the Scottish Kirk.
The Puritan movement flourished inside, not outside, the Anglican
Church; many Christians throughout England regarded themselves as
intensely conservative. They wanted preaching to become a more
central part of the Church services, they wished to pray to God after
their own fashion, and they required the communion service to be
purely commemorative. Above all, they honestly feared that the
King with his Roman Catholic wife and his Catholic Ministers, such
as the Lord Treasurer Portland and the Chancellor of the Exchequer
Francis Cottington, was conniving at the Catholicization of the
English Church. Yet Edward Hyde was to write that 'the imputation
raised by Parliament upon the King of an intention to bring in
Popery . . . did not make a deep impression on the people generally.'
Many of the diaries and memoirs of gentry who were to emerge as
Royalists — such as for example that of Dr Samuel Ward, the
introspective Master of Sidney Sussex College, Cambridge — exemp-
lify what may be called the Puritan habit of mind. They reveal a deep
consciousness of sin and a conviction of belonging to the Elect, of
intimacy with the Maker. Though some Puritans were more active
than others, notably those who, like Oliver Cromwell, the squire of
Ely, subscribed to the payment of lecturers — that is to say preachers
who composed their own sermons and did not read them from
prescribed books — the fact remains that by and large the bulk of the
kingdom was critical of the existing ecclesiastical authority. In the
House of Commons condemnation of Charles I's bishops, who paid
visitations throughout their sees to ensure ritualistic conformity, was
virtually unanimous.

The King thought it right to publish a long declaration to his
people as a whole after he dissolved Parliament on 10 March 1629.
Though he began by saying that 'princes are not bound to give
account of their actions but to God alone' he defended in detail his
domestic and religious policies. He justified the continued levying of
tonnage and poundage without parliamentary consent by appealing
to precedents from the reign of Edward IV and he insisted on his care
for religion, stating that he would never 'give way to the authorizing

of anything, whereby any innovation may steal or creep into the Church' but would preserve the unity of doctrine and discipline established in the time of Queen Elizabeth I. Thus the King as well as the Commons claimed to be conservative.

The day after Parliament adjourned in 1629 Sir John Eliot and eight other members of the House of Commons were summoned to appear before the Privy Council and on the following day were placed under arrest for conspiring sedition. All but three were eventually released on making their peace with the King, but the Court of King's Bench decided that Eliot and two others were guilty of a crime and could be kept in prison at the monarch's pleasure. It is said that Charles felt bitterly towards Eliot on the ground that his speeches in the Commons had incited the assassination of the Duke of Buckingham. Three years later Eliot was to die unhappily in the Tower of London. The harsh treatment of Eliot exacerbated the feelings of former members of parliament against Charles I.

The King managed to govern without Parliament because he reduced his expenses and increased his revenues. Peace was concluded with both France and Spain. The yield from Customs rose, reaching an average of £400,000 a year between 1636 and 1641; ship money was levied from both ports and inland towns and realized about £180,000 during the first year. The King also revived various feudal dues including fines on those who had encroached on the royal forests and those who created depopulation by enclosures of common land. Money could be borrowed fairly easily from the City of London. Financially therefore the Government kept its head above water. Altogether the King had about a million pounds a year at his disposal. His son was only to be voted £1,200,000 a year by a loyal Parliament.

It has been contended by apologists for Charles I that he adopted a paternalistic policy towards the poor, who were better off than if the House of Commons had been sitting. A Book of Orders was issued to make local government more effective, poor rates were reinforced by commissioners and efforts were exerted to find occupation for the unemployed. Roads and canals were built, fens were drained with the assistance of Dutch engineers and a postal service was established. But as has justly been observed, 'the way that government worked in the early seventeenth century meant that State intervention usually led to good profits for some individual or privileged group, paid for by giving the King his share' − as, for instance, in the fenland draining schemes. It is doubtful if any consistent domestic policy was followed. In any case Charles did not neglect his own comforts, notably his hobby of collecting pictures.

In religion the King continued to favour the so-called 'Arminians'. Laud gave instructions that in the churches in his diocese the altars were to be restored to the east end of the nave and he approved of the reissue of the Book of Sports which allowed amusements after services on Sundays, both moves calculated to offend the strict Puritans. Those who by word or deed repudiated the attempt to achieve religious uniformity were hauled before the Court of Star Chamber − a prerogative court − and could be punished severely. Laud had his good points. He genuinely believed in promoting a social policy favourable to the poor and he aimed to ensure the beauty of holiness by maintaining a standard of decency and order in parish churches. Thus he approved of the wearing of vestments by clergy and of the congregations bowing towards the altar. In 1633 before becoming Archbishop of Canterbury he accompanied Charles to Scotland where the King was crowned in Holyrood Palace. Because the Archbishop of Glasgow refused to wear a surplice at the ceremony, he was not allowed to take part in it. This visit alienated leading Lowland Scotsmen who hated both foreigners and Popery.

In that year too Laud's friend Thomas Wentworth was sent by the King to govern Ireland. Wentworth had earlier been highly critical of the monarchy and prominent in securing the passage of the Petition of Right through Parliament. But since the Petition had been accepted Wentworth entered the royal service and was created Viscount Strafford. After four years' work as Lord President of the North he was promoted to be Lord Deputy of Ireland where he carried out a programme of thorough political and economic reform, but did not omit to fill his own pockets. Charles's attitude to Wentworth was always cool, partly no doubt because of his past behaviour and partly because he did not like or really trust him. Laud, who was twenty years older than Wentworth, the King trusted, even if he did not always follow his advice. In fact a principal royal counsellor was the Roman Catholic Queen who gave birth to three sons and four daughters and to whom Charles became devoted.

Thomas Wentworth, Earl of Strafford (1593–1641), Lord Lieutenant of Ireland and one of the King's principal advisers in 1639–40. The King's signature on Strafford's death warrant after the passing of an Act of Attainder in 1641 weighed heavily on the monarch's conscience. The King had promised that he would not suffer in life, honour or estate, and his final defeat in the civil war and even his own execution were seen by Charles as divine retribution for this breach of faith. More than ten years earlier Strafford had prophesied: 'Whoever ravels forth into questions the right of a king and of a people shall never be able to wrap them up again into the comeliness and order he found them.'

He was once heard to say to her: 'I wish that we could always be together, and that you could accompany me to the Council.' Though that was not thought permissible, Henrietta Maria exerted her influence behind the scenes. As a Bourbon and a Medici, she was no lover of parliaments.

With Charles's revenues improving sufficiently for him to manage comfortably as long as his two kingdoms remained at peace, he might have been able to govern indefinitely without calling another Parliament. But in 1638 two events occurred which altered the entire situation. The first was the divided verdict of the twelve judges in the test case brought by John Hampden about the legality of ship money. This case focused the nation-wide dissatisfaction over the levy of the tax upon all English counties during an era of peace. The propaganda arising in consequence of the trial and the fact that only seven of the twelve judges found in favour of the King contributed to widespread resistance to payment of ship money in 1639–40. Attempts to confiscate property where the tax was refused resulted in the murder of one official and intense indignation among the poorer farmers, whose only cows were seized when they failed to meet their share of this taxation. The second event was the King's decision to impose a prayer book similar to the English liturgy upon the Scottish Kirk, which resulted in riots in Edinburgh, the drawing up of a National Covenant expressing the solidarity of the Scottish Lowlanders against English interference with their religious way of life, and the consequent resolve of Charles I that summer to prepare to enforce his will on his Scottish subjects by war.

The Church or Kirk had existed ever since 1567, the year in which Mary Queen of Scots had abdicated. Its doctrine was based on an extreme Calvinist position, embodied in a Confession of Faith, while the ecclesiastical organization in Scotland derived from a Book of Discipline which, unlike the Confession of Faith, had not been registered by the Scottish Parliament. In this reformed Kirk ministers were elected by their own congregations and discipline was entrusted to lay elders. Moreover the Kirk had been given the right by King James VI, when he succeeded his mother, to call General Assemblies which dealt with matters of religion and discipline. King James, however, believed that the Presbyterian system undermined the monarchy and he managed in 1600 to appoint four bishops to the

Kirk, though – partly because they had no ecclesiastical courts – they did not possess the disciplinary powers that English bishops enjoyed. Charles I was determined that uniformity of religion should prevail in his two kingdoms. Little did he realize the resentment that the new prayer book would arouse. 'What he was doing,' as Gardiner remarked, 'he did from a love of order, combined with sheer ignorance of mankind.' But this resentment was not created solely by his attempt to insist upon the use of the new prayer book at Easter 1637. The Scottish nobility were at one with the leaders of the Kirk in resisting the claims of the bishops both in Church and State. They were united in opposing a new regime, of which this liturgy was the symbol, being foisted upon them. The National Covenant was signed by most of the Scottish nation in defence of their Kirk.

In February 1638 Charles was personally warned by his Lord Treasurer in Scotland that if he wished the new prayer book to be used he would have to support it with 40,000 men in arms. In that very same month the Covenanters were celebrating 'the great marriage day of the nation with God'. From then on Charles played for time to achieve his ends. He realized that he could not possibly be ready for war before the spring of 1639. Therefore he told the Marquis of Hamilton, whom he had appointed as his Commissioner in Scotland, to allow the use of the prayer book to be suspended and to permit a General Assembly of the Kirk to be called. The Assembly, which met in Glasgow instead of Edinburgh, because Hamilton believed that his own influence was stronger there, proved unreceptive to blandishments and grew defiant. When Hamilton ordered its dissolution it refused to obey and after rejecting the new prayer book it abolished the bishops. Both sides prepared for war.

This civil war between Charles and his Scottish subjects was not fought over the question for which the King had first contended. What in fact happened was that the King had provoked a Scottish national movement against him led by Presbyterian ministers who induced the canny citizens of Edinburgh to unloose their purse-strings. Everything was organized with typical Scottish efficiency. Professional officers, who had returned from fighting in the Thirty Years War in Germany, trained the stout young ploughmen in the military arts. Though none of the Highland chieftains (most of whom were Roman Catholic) took part in the war except for the saturnine and dedicated Marquis of Argyll and his Campbells, the Lowlanders flocked to the colours. The King, on the other hand, lacked the funds with which to buy sufficient arms and supplies (for his revenues had contracted since the Hampden trial), while the militiamen from southern England who formed the bulk of his infantry had not their hearts in the northern war. Charles did however possess a small but splendid force of cavalry under the command of Lord Holland which crossed the border from Berwick on Tweed on Whit Monday 1639. But the mounted English soldiers recoiled before the vast lines of Scottish infantry. All Charles's advisers begged him to conclude peace. So he decided to abandon the campaign in the hope that the Scots would be divided in their allegiance and that he himself could raise a better army. By the Pacification of Berwick it was arranged that both armies should disband and that a Scottish Parliament and General Assembly should meet that autumn when the King himself would come to Edinburgh to complete a settlement.

The King never went to Edinburgh. On the contrary he regarded the agreement at Berwick as a mere truce. He thought that he had been unlucky in his first Scottish campaign. He had chosen the wrong commanders; he had failed to collect sufficient money; he had given in too soon: after all, the Scots had not actually fought against him. Therefore in the summer of 1639 he decided to send for his most successful servant, Viscount Strafford, his Lord Deputy in Ireland, to seek his advice and help. In fact Strafford had not approved of the Scottish war, not that he thought the King was wrong to assert his authority but because he considered that the whole operation was insufficiently prepared. Soon after Strafford arrived in London he combined with the Marquis of Hamilton and Archbishop Laud in pressing the King to summon a new Parliament at Westminster in order that he might obtain from it adequate supplies to wage war on the Scots. Surely loyal and patriotic Englishmen would rally to his assistance against their traditional enemies? Charles was always volatile. Strafford promised him money and troops from Ireland; the King hoped to raise a large loan in the City of London which had recently appointed a friendly Lord Mayor; he ordered the fortifications of Berwick on Tweed and Carlisle which guarded the main routes into Scotland to be strengthened and *the English and Scotts Armies at first ready to fight, lovingly embrace each other, & part kinde freinds,*

The Pacification of Berwick was used by the King as a stalling measure; his opponents saw it as a capitulation. This engraving presents the Parliamentarian view of the event.

organized the manufacture of weapons of war in English arsenals. He showed his confidence in Strafford by raising him to the post of Lord Lieutenant of Ireland and granting him the earldom after which he hankered. Moreover he accepted the advice he gave to call a Parliament in England. While the arrangements for its election were being undertaken, Strafford returned to Ireland to collect subsidies and soldiers for his King.

Strafford had been so successful in manipulating the Irish Parliament that he was confident that a carefully worded appeal to an English Parliament would arouse a ready and loyal response. After all, Sir John Eliot was dead, John Pym was ageing, the English never liked the Scots. Strafford himself had been a leading member of the House of Commons and thought that he knew how it could be managed. But he was living in a dream world.

As has been noticed, during the eleven years' intermission between Parliaments grievances had accumulated in the English counties and boroughs where members were chosen. It is possible that both the royal officials and the critics of the Government, who were grouped round the wealthy Earl of Warwick (Pym had been the Secretary of the Providence Company of which Warwick and John Hampden were shareholders), tried to do what they could to influence the elections. But it is more likely that, as usual, the county gentry agreed among themselves about who the members should be, while provision was made for a few royal officials to be chosen, such as Sir Henry Vane the Elder, who had recently been appointed Secretary of State. But the atmosphere of the time was all against the Court. A rhymester who wrote

> Choose no ship sheriff or court atheist
> No fen drainer nor church papist

probably reflected the current prejudices. At any rate when Parliament met at Westminster on 13 April and was asked by the Lord Keeper for a generous supply of funds as well as the legalization of tonnage and poundage so that the King might win a victory over the rebellious Scots, Pym demanded in a two-hour speech that the liberties and privileges of Parliament should first be attended to and the verdict given in the ship-money case be re-examined. Charles I offered to abandon ship money – which he was in fact no longer able to collect, so widespread was the discontent with it – if the Commons would vote him twelve subsidies (about £840,000). When after three weeks this offer was refused, the King dissolved what was to be known as the 'Short Parliament'.

The Earl of Strafford, who returned to London after a whirlwind visit to Ireland, did not approve of the decision to dissolve this Parliament; nor did Archbishop Laud. They believed that a compromise might have been reached and that their master was over-hasty. But tactful compromise was not one of Charles's characteristics. He resolved to renew the war against the Scots without parliamentary aid.

Strafford agreed that the war against the Scots must be resumed, but he and most of the royal counsellors were justifiably pessimistic about its result. Strafford himself was appointed Commander-in-Chief of the army, but he was laid low with dysentery, pleurisy and stone and had to be carried north in a litter. 'Never', he declared, 'came any man to so mightily lost a business.' This time the Scots did not wait to be invaded, but crossed the Tyne meeting little resistance. In humiliation the King was obliged to accept the Treaty of Ripon (21 October 1640) by which he agreed to allow the Scottish army to remain in Northumberland and Durham and to pay its expenses there until final terms were settled. Unjustly Charles blamed Strafford for the failure of his second campaign against the Scots. Now the King had no alternative but to call another Parliament to Westminster. The meeting of this Parliament – to be known as the Long Parliament – on 3 November 1640 led directly to the civil wars in England.

CHAPTER THREE

The War Opens:
1640–1642

No serious evidence has yet been discovered to prove that John Pym or anyone else campaigned to influence the character of the Parliament that met at Westminster in the late autumn of 1640. A historian who has examined the question closely writes: 'no band of revolutionaries were these, the men of England's revolutionary parliament'. It was composed, much in the way that the Short Parliament and other Parliaments had been, chiefly of leading country gentlemen, many of whom were related to one another. To give one or two examples: Denzil Holles, the member for Dorchester, who had been a strong opponent of ship money and was to become (until 1647) a critic of the King's Government, was the second cousin of Gervase Holles, a member for Grimsby, who was to show himself later to be a Royalist. Sir Edward Dering, a member for the county of Kent, who was also to become a Royalist, was related to Sir Henry Vane the Younger, in later years to emerge as a prominent republican. Bulstrode Whitelocke, the member for Great Marlow, by profession a lawyer, who was to figure importantly in the future republican administration, was related to Sir Edward Hyde, a member for Cornwall who was to be one of the most loyal adherents of Charles I and his son. But at the time nearly all of these men were well-to-do subjects and at first were equally critical of the King's policies. It has been estimated that not more than fifty members of the House of Commons were courtiers or royal officials, but even if they were, that did not necessarily mean that they approved the

King's domestic, foreign or religious programme. For instance, Sir Edmund Verney, who held the office of Knight Marshal of the Household and was to die fighting for the King, 'voted steadily in opposition to Charles's wishes'. At least nine-tenths of the Commons were critical of the King's 'evil counsellors'.

The general atmosphere of the time was one of restlessness and uncertainty brought about not only by a trade depression, unemployment and plague but also by the presence of the Covenanter army on English soil. In London the senior alderman, who was known to be loyal to the Government, was rejected as Lord Mayor in favour of a compromise candidate; the Recorder for London, whom the King wanted to be chosen Speaker of the House of Commons, was not elected a member of parliament for the City and all four City members were Puritans known to be highly critical of the Government. Yet the City officials as a whole were by no means disloyal; it was the London shopkeepers and apprentices and, as the King was to declare later, 'the meaner sorts of people' who first showed themselves to be disorderly and dissatisfied with the King's Government.

The King himself made the opening speech to Parliament in which he insisted that the Scots were rebels and that Parliament must provide money to pay for his army so as to get rid of the Scots. Charles I was aware that most of his Ministers were broken reeds. The Lord Keeper, Finch, in addressing the new Parliament, claimed that the Scottish war had been approved by the whole of the Privy Council and thus implicitly laid the blame for its initiation on the King himself. Charles had understandably called upon the Earl of Strafford, the only really strong man in his Privy Council, to come up to London to lend him his support. Strafford had no illusions about his task. When he left his home to go to Westminster on 6 November he declared that he was going to London 'with more danger beset, I believe, than ever man went out of Yorkshire'. He disapproved of Finch's speech and regarded it as his duty to defend the King's policy towards the Scots and face any charges that Pym and the Commons chose to bring against him. On the very day after Strafford took his seat in the House of Lords Pym announced his intention of impeaching him for treason. Other advisers of the King, including Laud, were also attacked as 'evil counsellors', but Strafford's case was

John Pym (1584–1643), here in a painted miniature by Samuel Cooper, was leader of parliamentary opposition to Charles I and his Government

deliberately selected as a trial of strength between the majority of the Commons and Charles I.

Though Strafford was thus the main objective of the movement against the Government and the strategy adopted by both sides was to make him the scapegoat, it must be understood that the accumulation of grievances since Charles I came to the throne and during the long intermission between Parliaments was what created an atmosphere of near unanimity in Parliament. In his speech Pym wove these grievances together and complained of attacks on parliamentary privileges, innovations in religion, and the invasions of the liberties of subjects by the enforcement of illegal taxation. It was the very breadth of these grievances that enabled Pym, in a House of Commons which contained many future Royalists, to keep the House united. Hyde, for example, as a practising lawyer, condemned the prerogative courts; Lord Falkland blamed the Bench of Judges for permitting the King to collect ship money; Sir Edward Dering was angry over clerical abuses; Sir John Culpeper stigmatized 'monopolists' as 'the frogs of Egypt' who 'sup in our cup, dip in our dish and sit by our fire'. But Pym was the man who held everything together. He realized that once the King's Ministers had been overthrown — and the mere threat of impeachment caused two or three of them to flee the country — the supremacy of Parliament would be established and the roots of monarchical power undermined.

Pym therefore refused to be diverted by questions of religious organization about which the Commons were not unanimous and managed to get a proposal to abolish the bishops, sponsored by Henry Vane the Younger and Oliver Cromwell, one of the members for Cambridge, put on one side. On the other hand, he approved of an attempt to legalize the regular meeting of Parliament; and a Bill requiring that Parliament should meet at least once every three years was read in the Commons for the third time in January 1641. It was during this same month that the detailed accusations against Strafford were presented by Pym and his colleagues before the House of Lords. Strafford's trial opened on 22 March, but he defended himself with such vigour and persuasiveness that it soon became doubtful whether the Lords would convict their fellow peer. Most of the charges against him could hardly be described as treasonable, while the evidence that he had given unconstitutional advice to the King was tenuous. By the middle of April Pym and his friends decided to proceed against Strafford not by impeachment but by promoting a Bill of Attainder condemning him to death as a traitor. The advantage of this procedure was that no proof of guilt was necessary; it was sufficient merely to assert that Strafford had severed the ancient harmony between the King and Parliament. The disadvantage of this method was that assent to the Bill would be required not only from the House of Commons (which passed it by a substantial majority) but also from the House of Lords and the King.

But they could be intimidated. It was the success of this intimidation that opened the direct road to civil war.

During the last week of April and the beginning of May the King and John Pym manoeuvred against each other. Charles assured Strafford that though he would have to dismiss him from the royal service he should not 'suffer in life, honour or fortune'. He then attempted to conciliate Strafford's opponents in the House of Lords by appointing them to the Privy Council. When that failed, he summoned the two Houses of Parliament to meet him. In a speech, which even his friends regarded as ill-judged, he insisted that his tender conscience would not allow him to agree to the attainder of Strafford; he appealed particularly to the House of Lords to rescue him from his embarrassment. But his speech made no impact and when next day Charles sent an officer with a hundred men to seize the Tower of London in which Strafford was lodged as a prisoner, the Lieutenant of the Tower, Sir William Balfour, defied his orders. Then the King and Queen thought of moving out of London to take refuge with the remnants of the royal army in the north of England. But as usual Charles was irresolute.

On the other side, City mobs agitated for Strafford's execution. A petition with thousands of signatures demanded the death of a traitor. The names of the minority in the Commons who had voted against the Bill of Attainder were posted up in the city and described as 'betrayers of their country'. Shops were shut; wild rumours circulated; an armed multitude accompanied the members of parliament when they went to ask the King to sign the Bill of Attainder.

Why did the House of Lords pass the Bill? Some members who might have voted against it were too frightened to appear, while others believed that if Strafford escaped, he would raise an army against Parliament. The King too began to fear for the safety of his Queen. He thought that armed mobs might invade his palaces of Whitehall and St James's – as the French mob was to surge into the palaces of Louis XVI a hundred and fifty years later. Strafford himself wrote to the King begging him to sign the Bill of Attainder so that harmony might be restored between him and his subjects. Judges assured Charles that Strafford had indeed been guilty of treason, while a bishop was found to draw a distinction between the King's private and public conscience. On 10 May Charles gave his assent to

THOMAS *Graaf van Straffort, Onder Koning van Ierland, Binnen Londen Onthalst. Den 22 van May 1641.*

Events in England were watched carefully from the continent. This is a Dutch engraving of the execution of the Earl of Strafford on 22 May 1641

The reign of Charles I heralded the first great age of portraiture in England. In 1632 the King appointed the Flemish Anthony Van Dyck as his principal painter in ordinary, knighted him, and paid him £200 a year. Van Dyck spent seven years in England, where he died in 1641 at the age of forty-two and was buried in St Paul's cathedral. His study of King Charles in three positions is one of his finest royal portraits; it was sent to Bernini in Rome as a model to be copied for a sculptured bust. Van Dyck's portraits of the King picture him as majestic and melancholy, but have been considered unduly flattering

PAINTED GLASS
IN A
WINDOW
OF
FARNDON CHURCH
Containing Portraits
of Cheshire Gentlemen
who attended K.Charles I.
at the Siege of Chester.

From a Drawing contributed by
the very Rev.Hugh Cholmondeley
Dean of Chester.

A painted glass window in the church at Farndon in Cheshire was put up after the Restoration to commemorate soldiers who fought in the King's army at Chester. As the main staging point from Ireland it was a strategic town. Chester was held by the Royalists throughout the first civil war and did not surrender to the Parliamentarians until February 1646 the Bill; and he signed another Bill for the perpetuation of the existing Parliament with the same pen and ink as he signed away the life of his Minister. Strafford was not even allowed to see his friend, Archbishop Laud, who was also imprisoned in the Tower, before being shepherded to the scaffold on 12 May. Laud himself wrote apropos the death of Strafford that the King 'knew not how to be or be made great'.

Two important questions arise out of the events in the spring of 1641 which were a dress rehearsal for the civil war. The first is of whom did the armed mobs consist that intimidated the King and Strafford's fellow peers into passing the Bill of Attainder? It seems that those who lined the approaches to Westminster Hall on the afternoon of 8 May were mainly respectable merchants, shopkeepers, members of the City of London militia, and apprentices. On the other hand, the crowds who gathered in Palace Yard and outside Whitehall Palace during the readings of the Bill were of a rougher character and included 'ordinary mechanic folk' from Southwark. Plainly when one talks of an armed multitude (unless one is thinking in terms of men simply armed with sticks and clubs) it is pretty certain that those who possessed swords or muskets were better-off citizens. It is likely that the demonstrations were actually organized by members of parliament for the City led by Isaac Penington, who were not only fiercely puritanical but were practising merchants influential with the shopkeepers and apprentices in the City companies. It was therefore an alliance between discontented members of the Commons and organized mobs which brought the King to his knees.

The second question is what did Pym and his friends hope to gain by compelling the King to abandon Strafford? Modern historians have concluded that on the whole Pym was loyal to the monarchy, true to the existing constitution, which he believed had been violated by the King's advisers, and in general was leader of a moderate party which aimed to uphold the prevailing structure of society. These moderates, it has been contended, were conservatives who only wanted to restore order in the Church and State as it had been in the good old days. Pym, wrote Gardiner, was 'purely conservative' and constituted himself 'the guardian of the old religion and the old law'. But the fact remained that his clear object was (however he may have phrased it) to strengthen the position of Parliament at the expense of the monarchy. Before he died he was not only to ensure the constitutional irremovability of the House of Commons in which he reigned supreme but also to require that the King surrender his power over the army and allow his Ministers to be approved by Parliament. Pym was not an emotional man; he was patient and deliberate in his behaviour and convinced that the House of Commons was or should be the soul of the body politic. As Veronica Wedgwood has justly observed, what men like Pym and his friends, John Hampden and Oliver St John, were aiming at was not merely the removal of Strafford and the King's other 'evil counsellors' but 'the transference of effective power from the King's hands into that of the High Court of Parliament'. They might refer back to the murky days of King John and his son for precedents, but in reality their aims were revolutionary.

'The summer of 1641', it has been said, 'was a time of play-acting and changes of mood.' Pym purposed to follow up his triumph against Strafford by introducing constitutional reforms and reducing the royal prerogatives. In order to do so he had to prevent quarrels arising between the two Houses of Parliament as well as stopping the Commons from sinking into a morass of private Bills and religious disputes. For his part the King hoped that if he continued to grant concessions a reaction would set in to his advantage. He might even be able to retain his rights by force, for he still had the army formed by Strafford in Ireland and his own army in the north of England; he might also be able to come to terms with the Covenanter army. Convinced that he ruled by divine right, he hoped that in God's own good time his former position of authority would be restored, if necessary by duress.

So during June and July Charles gracefully made concessions, He had already agreed that Parliament could not be dissolved without its own consent and that in future Parliaments would be called regularly, specific provisions being included in a Triennial Act which allowed Parliament to be summoned without the King's orders. Tonnage and poundage were in future to be voted only for very short periods and the yield from these duties was to be kept under the close supervision of the Commons. Ship money was declared illegal. Money voted for the payment of the Scottish army was not to be

Robert Devereux, 3rd Earl of Essex (1591–1646), who was appointed Lord General of the Parliamentarian army. This portrait of him is attributed to Daniel Mytens handed over to the Treasury, but paid directly to the City of London which had raised a loan for the purpose of its upkeep. Conciliar jurisdiction was thenceforward abolished in all its forms: this meant that both the Court of Star Chamber, instituted by the Tudors to deal with over-powerful subjects, and the High Commission, which was created to sustain the authority of the Church, now ceased to exist. The King repudiated friends of his who both in England and Scotland concocted or tried to concoct military plans on his behalf. Furthermore he promoted the third Earl of Essex, an enthusiastic Puritan who had been active in hounding Strafford to his death, to be his Lord Chamberlain.

How far the King really followed any consistent policy at this stage has been disputed. It has been asserted that he oscillated between concessions and intrigues. What does seem pretty clear is that he regarded everything he yielded under pressure from the House of Commons as indulgences conferred while he was playing for time to win back his authority. In assenting to the Triennial Bill, for example, he said that 'never a Bill passed here was of more favour to subjects than this is', but added, 'you have taken the government all in pieces and I may say off its hinges. . .'. This was the kind of language to arouse suspicions and increase the influence of those who still felt that Charles was not to be trusted. But on the other hand at the same time the campaign of religious extremists – as exemplified by a 'root-and-branch' Bill put forward to abolish bishops and deans as well as an attempt that was made to exclude bishops from the House of Lords – not only alienated peers, as trenching upon their historic rights, but antagonized moderate members of the Church such as Lord Falkland and Edward Hyde in the Commons. These men cannot yet be described as Royalists, but they were coming to believe that constitutional reform had gone far enough; they genuinely wanted to reconcile monarchy and Parliament; and they themselves were willing to accept ministerial offices, thus becoming the agents of such a reconciliation.

But Pym clung to a more revolutionary point of view. When the King announced that he had decided to visit Scotland early in August after a settlement had at last been reached with the Covenanters, the Commons not only set up a committee to supervise the defence of the realm, but selected a number of Commissioners to follow Charles to

Scotland, that is to say in effect to spy upon his movements. When Parliament adjourned for six weeks the two Houses appointed a committee, over which Pym himself presided, to manage business during the recess, to arrange for the demobilization of the King's army, and to keep in touch with the Commissioners sent to Scotland. Moreover Pym and his friends were now determined to ensure the expansion of parliamentary authority not merely while the Houses were in recess but for all time by claiming the right to nominate or approve all the king's Ministers and military officers.

Parliament reassembled on 20 October 1641 while the King was still in Scotland graciously bestowing concessions on all and sundry. Within a fortnight members learned the news that a rebellion had broken out in Ulster where the native Irish seized arms, plundered the English settlers and threatened to advance on Dublin, partly because they feared that it was the intention of the Lord Justices, who had ruled there since the death of Strafford, to extirpate the Roman Catholic religion and partly because they were provoked by hatred of intruders who kept them ground down by poverty. At Westminster Pym grasped the opportunity provided by grossly exaggerated stories of Irish massacres, which he blamed on the incompetence of the King's Ministers and the Catholic predilections of the Court, to put forward his own panacea. On 5 November he moved that unless Charles agreed to dismiss those of his counsellors who were at fault and replace them with advisers approved by Parliament, the Commons should offer no assistance in suppressing the Irish rebellion. On the following day Oliver Cromwell moved that the Earl of Essex should be empowered by 'an ordinance of Parliament' and not by the instructions of the monarch to take command of the English militia in order to defend the kingdom and that he should continue to do so until Parliament decided otherwise. Thus the House of Commons endorsed two far-reaching propositions: first, that the King should 'employ only such counsellors and ministers as should be approved by Parliament'; secondly, that Parliament and not the King should supervise the defence of the realm.

Pym's motion that the King should only employ Ministers approved by Parliament was carried in the Commons by 151 votes to 110. Immediately afterwards Pym introduced a 'Grand Remonstrance' in which all the grievances against the Government during

The panic aroused by the Irish rebellion of 1641–2 was reflected in a number of prints and pamphlets published in London by Puritan sympathizers. This map of Ireland (*c.* 1642) is believed to distinguish between 'the Townes revolted, taken or burnt' during the rebellion

Charles I's reign were listed as a manifesto to the nation; not only were all the past political failures set out – for example, wars mis-managed by Buckingham – but the assertion was made that the 'fundamental laws' of the kingdom had been undermined and a Popish conspiracy fomented to divide the King from his people. In the debates on the Remonstrance the main opposition was displayed over the religious clauses. Edward Hyde did not deny that the catalogue of grievances was true, but he considered that to rehash their history was pointless and tactless. Some members thought that it was ridiculous to say that the Book of Common Prayer contained superstitions; and others denied that bishops were idolaters. Eventually the Remonstrance was approved on 22 November by a mere 159 votes to 148. Oliver Cromwell declared that had it not been passed he and other members would have left England for ever.

The House of Commons consisted of over five hundred members: out of that number only three hundred steadily attended the debates. The votes in November showed that the three hundred were almost equally divided over questions of politics and religion. But the leaders of the majority maintained that it was iniquitous to suggest that the House was divided at all; was it not a Great Council of the Realm comparable to the seamless robe of Christ? Two men were actually sent to the Tower for admitting that there were 'two sides' in the House. Yet it was absurd to pretend otherwise. Charles I, when he returned to London from Scotland three days after the Grand Remonstrance was carried, recognized the obvious situation and for that reason was at last emboldened to stand firmly for his rights. He was welcomed by the official authorities in the City of London, which now had a Lord Mayor friendly to him. As if to emphasize his aloofness he retired to the Tudor palace of Hampton Court outside London where he was visited by a deputation from the majority in the Commons who invited him to accept the Remonstrance and let Parliament henceforward approve his Ministers. The King retorted by depriving the Earl of Essex of his post of Commander-in-Chief, relieving the London militia of the duty of guarding Parliament, replacing it with loyal halberdiers under the Earl of Dorset, and on 21 December removing Balfour from the lieutenancy of the Tower. He also issued a declaration on religion, upholding the Book of Common Prayer, and named new bishops to fill empty sees.

This challenge to Parliament or resumption of the royal authority was met by a fresh demonstration by Penington and his friends in the City. After an armed demonstration gathered at Westminster on 29 November crying out 'No Popery!' it was firmly dealt with by the Earl of Dorset. When a fortnight later a petition was brought from the City demanding the exclusion of the bishops from the House of Lords and asking that the control over the militia be transferred from the King to Parliament, only a hundred petitioners were allowed into the House of Commons to put their case. On 10 December the Commons again revealed their divisions, for the motion to take away the control of the militia from the King was carried by 158 votes to 125. The King saw his chance. On 14 December he came to the House of Lords to say that he would only pass the Militia Bill if his rights were respected. On 23 December he in effect rejected the Grand Remonstrance passed in the Commons (which, much to his annoyance, had been printed); he stood by the Church of England and the traditional rights of the English monarchy. Thus were the lines of battle clearly drawn.

The crux came during the twelve days of Christmas. Agitations swept the City. The stairs from the River Thames to Palace Yard were crowded with citizens who aimed to prevent bishops from landing there to take their seats in the House of Lords. Apprentices flooded Whitehall. The King, though giving way to protests over the lieutenancy of the Tower, saw that it stayed in the hands of a man he could trust. Finally Charles made up his mind to impeach Pym and four other members of the Commons together with one member of the House of Lords – Lord Mandeville (the future Earl of Manchester and Parliamentarian commander) – for treason. The majority of the peers, though sympathetic to the King, doubted his claim to impeach: indeed it was thought to be a violation of their own rights. Therefore his request that they should order the arrest of members of parliament was refused. On 4 January 1642 Charles decided to act on his own responsibility. But by the time he entered the House of Commons that evening, had taken off his hat, and occupied the Speaker's chair, the five accused members had departed by barge down the river. Their friends hid them safely in the heart of the City. Six days later, realizing that he had been outmanoeuvred, the King removed his family from Whitehall to Hampton Court. He was not

1 You ar to accuse those ~~three~~ *five* joynthe & severalue

2 you ar to referue the power of making additionally

3 When the (omitie for examination is a naming (wch you must press to be close & under tey of secresie) if eather Essex, Warwick, Holland, Say, ████████ Wharton, or Brooke be named, you must desyre that they may be spared because you ar to examine them as witnesses for me

King Charles's instructions to his Attorney-General, Sir Edward Hebert, for the impeachment of leading members of parliament, 3 January 1642

to return to London until he himself was put on trial seven years later.

When did the civil war become inevitable? Notions on inevitability are best left to predestinarians. What is sure is that preparations for war began as soon as the King left London. In January Charles ordered the Earl of Newcastle to assume the governorship of the port of Hull; he also tried to obtain control of Portsmouth and of the Tower of London and aimed to lay hold of the Surrey magazine at Kingston upon Thames. On 23 February the Queen secretly left England, nominally to attend the wedding of her daughter Mary in Holland, but in reality to pawn Crown jewels with which to buy arms. But John Pym, now known as 'King Pym', was extremely vigilant and frustrated all the royal plans except that he could not

Hampton Court, the Tudor palace outside London to which Charles withdrew with his
family in January 1641, and where he was held prisoner in 1647. Later, Cromwell used
the palace as his country residence when he was Lord Protector

prevent the Queen's departure. On 12 February the two Houses of
Parliament agreed upon a list of persons whom they recommended as
Lord-Lieutenants of the counties. The principal duty of these officers
was to concern themselves with the recruiting of the militia and
questions of local defence. To make assurance doubly sure three days
later an ordinance was introduced into the House of Commons
whereby the control of the militia was to be transferred from the
King to Parliament.

Though each side was thus already preparing for war, negotiations
between Parliament and the King continued until March. On
13 February Charles actually gave his assent to a Bill to exclude the
bishops from the House of Lords; he also promised to enforce the
penal laws against Roman Catholics and he agreed to a Bill
impressing soldiers to go to Ireland. The Queen had been largely
responsible for inducing her husband to make these concessions,
hoping that they would buy time while she was away. But she had
also insisted that the King should not on any account give up his
control over the militia. He made that clear in an interview with the
Earl of Pembroke at the end of February. Asked to agree to
abandoning his control temporarily, Charles answered 'By God, not

for an hour'. The preamble to the Militia Ordinance drawn up in the Commons affirmed that 'the High Court of Parliament is not only the Court of Judicature, enabled by the laws to adjudge and determine the rights and liberties of the Kingdom . . . but is likewise a Council to provide for the necessity, to prevent the imminent dangers, and preserve the public peace and safety of the kingdom'. Thus by March the two constitutional positions had been plainly defined. The King refused to give up his prerogatives; Parliament sought ultimate authority. By 22 March the Militia Ordinance had been passed by both Houses, the claim being asserted that it was valid without the royal assent. The question of the power of the sword was the breaking point in a contest of wills which stretched over two years.

By May the King had set up his headquarters in York where he summoned peers, judges and members of parliament to join him, and early in June Commissioners from Westminster carried their peace terms known as 'the nineteen propositions' to him there. These propositions demanded the right of Parliament to approve the King's Ministers, officials and judges; they required the King to agree to Parliament's plan for reforming the Church; and they asked for complete control of the militia and the castles and fortresses throughout the kingdom together with the dismissal of his personal guards. To this ultimatum, which in effect claimed supreme authority for Parliament and left the King as a figurehead, Charles answered by adopting the attitude that there should be a partnership between him and Parliament. For in reply he adumbrated a doctrine known as 'mixed monarchy' which would have been extremely distasteful to his father. He and his propagandists insisted that he did not seek absolute power or 'an arbitrary way of government' but merely a reversion to the ancient constitution under which the country was governed by the King in Parliament.

The nineteen propositions and the King's answer to them comprised a battle of words that led nowhere. In July Parliament appointed the Earl of Warwick to take command of the navy and the Earl of Essex to be general of a Parliamentarian army. The best that the King could do was to seize the port of Newcastle upon Tyne, to borrow money from some wealthy peers, and to issue commissions of array in the hope of recruiting soldiers in defiance of the arrangements being carried out on behalf of Parliament. As early as March

William Cavendish, Earl, Marquis and later 1st Duke of Newcastle (1593–1676), was one of the richest men in England. His appointment as Governor of Hull was one of Charles's first acts in preparation for civil war. Newcastle commanded the Royalist forces in the north until 1644, and withdrew abroad after the defeat at Marston Moor the recruiting efforts undertaken by rival Lord-Lieutenants in Lancashire resulted in the spilling of blood at the small town of Manchester. Parliament had already set up a Committee of Safety, composed of members of both Houses, to defend the kingdom against the King. Charles retorted by calling upon his loyal subjects to restore his authority. On 22 August the royal standard was formally raised in Nottingham and the civil war began.

CHAPTER FOUR

First Campaigns: 1642–1643

'On the whole,' wrote Gardiner a hundred years ago, 'the nobility and gentry took the side of the King, whilst townsmen and yeomanry took the side of Parliament.' Historians have been elaborating on that text ever since. We have seen that though the generalization can be sustained to a limited extent by literary evidence, close examination of county histories proves conclusively that the civil war was not a class war. The Earls of Bedford, Essex, Manchester, Northumberland, Pembroke, Peterborough and Warwick all served Parliament and all except Pembroke held high military commands. Though a majority of peers understandably sympathized with the King, the gentry were divided down the middle. To give a few examples: among the gentry of Cornwall Lord Robartes, Sir Richard Buller and Edmund Prideaux were for Parliament, Sir Francis Godolphin, Sir John Arundel and Sir Charles Trevanion were for the King. In Kent Sir Anthony Weldon, Sir Michael Livsey and Sir John Sedley were for Parliament, while Sir John Culpeper, Sir Roger Twysden and Sir Edward Dering were for the King. In Somerset Alexander Popham, John Pyne and William Strode – all well-to-do landlords – were keen Parliamentarians, while Sir Ralph Hopton, Sir John Poulett and Sir John Stawell were active Royalists.

Even families were not united in their loyalties. Writing for the benefit of his descendants, Sir John Oglander, a Royalist in the Isle of Wight, observed: 'Thou wouldst think it strange if I should tell thee there was a time in England when brothers killed brothers, cousins,

cousins and friends their friends.' That was literally true. Charles Fleetwood, a leading Parliamentarian officer, had a brother, Walter, who was a faithful Royalist; Sir Richard Feilding, who held Reading for the King in 1643, had an elder brother, Basil, who was fighting for Parliament. Sir Henry Vane, who was to become a dyed-in-the-wool republican, had a younger brother, Walter, who was a Royalist. Ralph Verney was told by his brother, Sir Edmund, the Knight Marshal of the King's Household, that his being against the King was 'most unhandsomely done' and that he regretted he must be his brother's enemy. Denzil Holles, a defiant and wealthy critic of the monarchical Government's policies in Church and State, had three cousins who were Royalists. In Yorkshire Sir Thomas Mauleverer raised three regiments for Parliament and was to sign the King's death warrant, but his son Richard fought for Charles and was imprisoned for his loyalty. Two commanders who fought on opposite sides during the war, Sir Ralph Hopton of Somerset and Sir William Waller, a Devonian, had been close friends and confessed that they were fighting 'a war without an enemy'.

The rich were not necessarily on the King's side. Although he was supported by two fabulously wealthy peers, the Earl of Newcastle and the Marquis of Worcester, it was on the whole in the poorer parts that most Royalists were to be found. It is dangerous to be too emphatic about the political complexion of the counties. While it is true that on the whole the west of England, the west Midlands, the East Riding of Yorkshire and the far northern counties were Royalist, while the home counties, eastern and south-eastern England were Parliamentarian, that was not always because of public opinion but because of the complications of regional affairs and family rivalries; moreover changes of attitude might be brought about by military pressures from without or changes in the fortunes of war within. For instance, Somerset was said to be Parliamentarian in 1642 and Royalist in 1643, largely because of an invasion from Cornwall. On the other hand, Kent was Royalist in 1642 and became Parliamentarian by 1643 in consequence of a military expedition dispatched there from Westminster. London itself – at any rate official London – was still Royalist during the first half of 1642, but by August 1643, owing to a *coup d'état* in the City, engineered from the House of Commons which impeached the Royalist Lord Mayor, it became

Sir William Waller (1597–1668), painted here by Sir Peter Lely, was one of the most able Parliamentarian commanders

Parliamentarian in sympathy and remained so for ten years or more.

Finally, it should be noted that the ports and towns in the kingdom and the merchant princes of the time were not necessarily Parliamentarian. When the war began Portsmouth, Newcastle and Chester, three busy ports, were under Royalist control. London, as has been noticed, was divided in its allegiance, while Bristol changed sides as a result of military action in 1643. Such merchants as had seats in the House of Commons, usually as representatives of boroughs, were equally divided in their loyalties; though some London financiers backed Parliament in 1642 because they resented the levying of Customs duties by the Crown without Parliament's consent, they were soon to discover that direct and indirect taxes introduced by 'King Pym' were heavier than anything that King Charles had imposed; by the end of the Interregnum the City was pretty solidly Royalist.

Since the beginning of 1642 both sides had been recruiting and collecting supplies. On paper the army serving under the Earl of Essex was formidable. Essex himself owed his position as much to his title as to the experience he acquired through having served in the Netherlands. He was a proud, indolent and melancholy man. As to his skill as a general, it has justly been pointed out by a modern military critic that he managed to fight three battles in positions where his enemy had cut him off from his base. (Cromwell also was to do so at the battle of Dunbar, but there his forces could be supplied by sea.) Charles I was his own commander-in-chief; his abilities have been underestimated. At least he had the right ideas, but he was a poor judge of men. He relied unduly upon cautious and aged professionals like Lord Forth. He never entirely trusted his brilliant young nephew, Prince Rupert of the Palatinate, who though only twenty-three was already an experienced soldier and came over to England at the start of the civil war to aid his uncle. Charles was to give him misleading orders and unjustified reprimands. The Earl of Essex had at his disposal six cavalry regiments, nineteen regiments of infantry and five troops of dragoons or mounted infantry, altogether some 15,000 men. On both sides an infantry regiment numbered or was supposed to number about 1,200 men and a cavalry regiment 300 or 400 men. Infantry regiments had both musketeers and

Charles I, standing in full armour, dictates to his Secretary-at-War Sir Edward Walker, who improvises with the use of a regimental drum as a writing desk. The setting is thought to be the country around Nottingham, where the King raised his standard at the beginning of the civil war

pikemen armed with clumsy weapons. The cavalry were heavy rather than light, wore armour and were relatively well paid; their action determined the result of most battles. As to the artillery, the heavy field-guns fired only about twelve times an hour and rarely played a significant part in the war except at sieges.

At the outset of the war the King had eight cavalry regiments, fifteen regiments of infantry and one of dragoons, a total of some 13,500 men, but the regiments were rarely up to strength. By the time that the battle of Naseby was fought in 1645 twenty of the so-called northern regiments serving the King had an average of only a hundred men each. To begin with the Royalist cavalry were better equipped and better trained than those of the Parliamentarians.

Warwick Castle was a parliamentary stronghold throughout the civil war

Neither side had much initial difficulty over recruiting, for 1642 was a year of depression and men enlisted for money as well as excitement. But discipline was poor on both sides. For though such professional officers as there were (who had mostly learned their trade abroad, some of them simply as volunteers in search of adventure) recognized the necessity of training in skirmishing as well as in drill. The first campaign began suddenly at an unusual time of the year when the harvests were still being brought in. Thus few opportunities occurred for more than rudimentary preparations; only the eight regiments of the London militia had undergone thorough training. Moreover when the war broke out a number of officers were still awaiting their commissions before they could start recruiting and exercising their men.

One other important factor was that the whole of the navy on which Charles had lavished the proceeds of the unpopular ship money declared itself for Parliament. In January 1642 2,000 mariners had marched into London to offer their services to Parliament. They were partly motivated by fear of Popery. In a protestation they referred to the 'rocks of Rome' and the 'quicksands of Spain', but no doubt the King's failure to pay his seamen punctually and regularly also alienated them from him. However, it is doubtful whether command of the sea was a decisive influence on the course of the first civil war, though it certainly was in the second and third civil wars. It was significant only in a negative sense: for had the royal navy been true to the King, he might have blockaded London and thus forced it into submission. As it was, Parliament's hold on the capital was crucial to its ultimate success in the civil wars.

Before the first battle of the war was fought both sides manoeuvred for position. On 13 September Charles left Nottingham and a week later arrived at Shrewsbury. Thence he darted north to secure Chester where troops from Ireland might be landed. Meanwhile the Earl of Essex had left London on 9 September, 'carrying with him his coffin and winding-sheet, together with the escutcheon which would be needed at his funeral', to reach Northampton four days later with a sizeable army. Two days afterwards he moved west and occupied Worcester on 21 September. Essex had originally hoped to confront the King at Nottingham and compel him to return to Westminster, but ill-founded rumours diverted him to Worcester. What in fact had happened was that a small Royalist force under Sir John Byron had arrived there from Oxford and Prince Rupert, also with a small body of horse, had ridden to meet him. A parliamentary detachment under Nathaniel Fiennes, sent in advance by the Earl of Essex, was surprised and beaten up. Fiennes was no soldier and his troopers were raw. The skirmish raised Royalist morale. But King Charles believed that the Parliamentarian army outnumbered his own and each army felt its way cautiously.

The Royalists then sought to move towards London, avoiding towns like Coventry, known to be garrisoned by Parliamentarians, while Essex advanced on a line parallel to that of the King southwards from Worcester and west of the line of the Royalist march. As Edward Hyde, who accompanied the King, wrote afterwards, though 'the two armies were but twenty miles asunder

The 2 of May, 1643. y* Croſſe in Cheapeſide was pulled
downe, a Troope of Horſe & 2 Companies of foote wayted
to garde it & at y* fall of y* tope Croſſe dromes beat tru-
pets blew & multitudes of Capes wayre throwne
in y* Ayre, & a greate Shoute of People with ioy,
y* 2 of May the Almana- ke ſayeth, was y* invention
of the Croſſe. & 6 day at night was the Leaden
Popes burnt, in the pla- -ce where it ſtood with
ringinge of Bells, & a greate Acclamation &
no hurt done in all these actions.

The 'idolatrous Cross' of Cheapside was pulled down on 2 May 1643, to the sound of
trumpets and 'a great shoute of people with joy'. This etching by Hollar was published
in John Vicars' *Sight of the Transactions of these latter yeares*, published in London in 1646.
A few days later, the *Book of Sports*, which had been reissued by Charles I, was burnt by
the hangman on the spot where the cross had stood

when they set forth and both marched the same way they gave not the
least disquiet in ten days march to each other; and in truth, as it
appeared afterwards, neither side knew where the other was'. On
Saturday 22 October the King was contemplating a halt at Edgecote
(forty miles west of Bedford) while a detachment occupied Banbury.
But that night Charles received a message from Prince Rupert that
the Earl of Essex was on his track and indeed that the enemy army

67

was only seven miles to his west. Next morning the King ordered his own army to occupy Edgehill which dominated the Warwickshire plain.

Rupert, whom the King had appointed as his General of Horse, immediately showed himself to be the most energetic of the royal officers and military advisers. He had already begun training the cavalry; he had raided Leicester to collect money for the King, an action which was at once disapproved; he had demonstrated his resource at Powick Bridge, where Fiennes had been surprised; he had acted as leader of a reconnaissance force during the advance south; and it was he who suggested the occupation of Edgehill. But being young, he was tactless. He insisted on receiving his orders directly from the King, thus upsetting the overall commander or General-in-Chief Lord Lindsey; furthermore Charles ordered Lord Forth, a veteran Scottish officer, to draw up the army ready for battle, whereupon Lindsey resigned to fight and die as a mere colonel. Undoubtedly the hope was that Essex would launch his forces uphill against the royal army; but it seems that Essex wanted the King to strike first so that he might be saddled with the blame for starting full-scale hostilities. The Royalists, who were extremely confident, were therefore obliged to move under the cover of cannon-fire down from Edgehill into the plain where they were redeployed. The battle began in the afternoon when Essex ordered his guns to open fire.

The two armies were roughly equal in size, though the Royalists were slightly stronger in cavalry. Officers then had neither watches nor adequate maps. Consequently it was extremely difficult to synchronize attacks once the trumpets had sounded the advance. This consideration applied to all the battles of the civil wars and it explains why overall commanders could plan their tactics only along very general lines; once the fighting began they had to rely on their subordinate officers to act as best they could. At Edgehill Rupert, who commanded the Royalist right wing – on each side both wings consisted of cavalry, with the infantry massed in the centre – bore down steadily, sword in hand, on the Parliamentarians opposite him; they vainly discharged their carbines and received little help from small groups of infantry who, after the Swedish fashion, were interspersed between their squadrons. The fury of the charge carried the Royalists too far forward under the mistaken impression that

PARLIAMENTARIANS

J.M. Sir John Meldrum's Brigade
C.E. Charles Essex's Brigade
T.B. Thomas Ballard's Brigade
W.F. Sir William Fairfax's Regiment
D.H. Denzil Holles' Regiment

  1. Lord Fielding's Regt.
  2. Sir Philip Stapleton's Regt.
  3. Sir William Balfour's Regt.
  4. Sir James Ramsey's Wing

ROYALISTS

H.W. Henry Wentworth
N.B. Sir Nicholas Byron
R.F. Richard Fielding
J.B. John Belasyse
C.G. Charles Gerard
J.U. James Usher's Dragoons

1. Lord Wilmot's Regt.	7. Prince Rupert's Regt.
2. Lord Grandison's Regt.	8. Prince of Wales' Regt.
3. Earl of Carnarvon's Regt.	9. King's Lifeguard
4. Lord Digby's Regt.	10. Sir John Byron's Regt.
5. Sir Thomas Aston's Regt.	11. Gentlemen Pensioners
6. Prince Maurice's Regt.	12. William Legge's Firelocks

––·–– Contours in metres above mean sea level.

Deployment of forces at the battle of Edgehill

The BATTLE
of
EDGE-HILL.

A dramatic, stylized representation of the battle of Edgehill, published late in the
seventeenth century

70

Diary entry by the Dutch engineer Sir Bernard de Gomme, after the battle of Edgehill. De Gomme had been brought to England by Prince Rupert, and he was a staunch supporter of the Royalists throughout the war. His account of 23 October 1642 reads in part: 'A fight between the Kings and Parliamt. forces att Keynton [Kineton] Marsh by Edgehill . . . Many sore wounded on both sides . . .'

their enemy was everywhere in retreat. Many of the Royalist troopers engaged in pillaging the Parliamentarians' baggage train three miles to the rear in the village of Kineton. The Royalist charge on the left was equally successful and again the troopers swept on to Kineton. Rupert managed to halt three of his troops and on the left Lieutenant-Colonel Sir Charles Lucas rallied 200 other cavalrymen. But these were by no means sufficient in number to come to the decisive help of the infantry which was engaged in a stiff struggle with the Parliamentarians in the centre. Some untrained parliamentary soldiers panicked; the musketeers were of little use; but massed 'hedgehogs' of pikemen fought hard and bravely. In the end these infantrymen, materially assisted by the intact cavalry regiment of Sir William Balfour, which had been held in reserve and thus avoided the charge on the left, thrust the Royalist foot soldiers back towards Edgehill and put the artillery out of action. Only the belated return of Prince Rupert's cavalry to the field of battle and the active intervention of the King himself prevented the cavalry victory from being transformed into an infantry defeat. Finally, as it grew dark, both sides were too exhausted to continue fighting. The two armies encamped on the field, but next day the Royalists returned to their original positions on Edgehill while the Earl of Essex retired to Warwick, his rearguard still harassed by Rupert's cavalry. Technically and actually, therefore, it was a Royalist victory.

Two lessons were learned from the battle of Edgehill. First, the Parliamentarians realized that the King had, after all, been able to recruit a substantial and capable army. The idea that once Charles had been confronted by an armed force raised and financed by Parliament he would be obliged to return to Westminster and accept the peace terms dictated to him had to be abandoned. Thus the decision was taken to reopen negotiations and at the same time to try to persuade a Scottish army to enter the north of England as allies of Parliament. Such persuasion, however, would take time. Secondly, the King understood what war meant. Casualties had been heavy; he had seen loyal officers like Sir Edmund Verney and the Earl of Lindsey die; so he too would have liked an accommodation.

After the battle both Rupert and Lord Forth, whom Charles had appointed as his General-in-Chief in place of Lindsey, urged the King immediately to undertake a forced march on London and compel Parliament to capitulate. He was dissuaded from doing so largely on political grounds, regarding it as a violent action which would alienate too many of his subjects. Instead on 29 October he entered Oxford, which was to remain his headquarters throughout the first civil war; then on 4 November he occupied Reading, while Rupert vainly tried to storm Windsor Castle, having already plundered Broughton Castle near Banbury, which had surrendered to the Royalists on 27 October. So it was not until nearly three weeks after Edgehill that the royal army arrived north-west of London.

Meanwhile the Earl of Essex with the remnants of his army had crossed the Chiltern Hills to reach the capital a week ahead of Rupert. Essex was received as a victor and voted £5,000 as a token of esteem, but he and his officers were fully aware that they had been beaten.

On 12 November Rupert arrived at Brentford on the north side of the River Thames and, aided by a mist, surprised and occupied the town. He then advanced on Turnham Green to the east on the route to the City, but he had shot his bolt. Mainly through the efforts of John Pym and with the aid of the London trained bands, the Earl of Essex had at his command a determined army of 24,000 men. On the other side, the King's army was tired after its long march south and was short of supplies. Charles had characteristically vacillated; for he had neither earnestly pursued peace negotiations in which terms favourable to him might conceivably have been reached nor had he struck hard enough or quickly enough with a victorious army. The Parliamentarians were able to assert that the King had acted treacherously in permitting the attack on Brentford when he had in fact agreed to open negotiations. Moreover the military threat to London and the plundering which Rupert had allowed at Brentford angered and frightened people and united the City behind Pym. So the Royalists recoiled and retreated.

While King Charles was retiring to Oxford the City of London authorities volunteered to raise an additional force of cavalry, while an Ordinance imposing a property tax or assessment on the population of London and Westminster was passed by the House of Commons. A week later this assessment was extended throughout all the English counties which were under parliamentary control. At first resentment over this new imposition was expressed in the City, which had been generous enough to the cause of Parliament. But learning of Royalist successes elsewhere, the City authorities acquiesced. A new loan of £60,000 was made to Parliament; the assessment was formalized at 5 per cent on all property; and two months later Pym proposed the introduction of an excise tax (modelled on that of the Dutch) which in the end was also reluctantly accepted. What with the assessments, the excise and the sequestration of Royalist property wherever it could be seized Parliament accumulated a war chest sufficient to pay for the upkeep of its army and navy. Charles had to depend on voluntary loans, on contributions

According to some sources, William Walker, who was wounded in the arm at Edgehill, died in 1736 at the age of 123

levied from the country round Oxford, and on the money which the Queen had succeeded in borrowing in Holland. In the long run the superiority of Parliament's financial resources was to assure the winning of the war.

During 1643 the fighting was fragmented over a number of different fronts – in Yorkshire, in East Anglia, in the west and south-west of England, and in the area round Oxford. Each side had been taken aback by its failure to achieve a striking blow in the previous autumn which might have made its enemy submit. Furthermore peace negotiations broke down because the demands put before the King by Parliament were too onerous for him. Though these negotiations continued spasmodically until March, neither side yielding an inch, fighting was already being resumed in earnest.

Over the past century nearly all historians have stated that in 1643 the King planned a grand strategy comprising a three-pronged thrust on London. The Earl of Newcastle, the King's General in Yorkshire, was to advance through East Anglia (hardly the quickest route to the capital); the King's army in the south-west, consisting chiefly of Cornishmen, was to move on London from the south; then the King's largest army, based on Oxford, was to launch the final assault on the capital. But there is not a shred of evidence that Charles had any such grand strategy in mind except for a story related by the Venetian representative in London to his master, the Doge, which was brought to him apparently by a servant of the King, who had formerly taught the Queen's Maids of Honour how to dance. Even that story merely stated that after the two first armies had closed upon each side of the Thames, the King aimed to 'scour the country with his cavalry', reducing London to extremities for food, and thus inducing the people to revolt against Parliament. Nothing was said about a 'final assault' on London. In fact the King had already missed his chance after the victory at Edgehill by refusing immediately to advance on the capital. He was then afraid that rather than ending the war at a blow the teeming population of the great city would turn more vehemently against him, as in fact its inhabitants did when they swarmed to Turnham Green to defy Prince Rupert. No doubt it is true that ultimately the war was likely to end with the surrender of either London or Oxford but that is no more than a military truism. The war might equally have ended with a decisive battle in any part of the kingdom.

If either side boasted a grand strategy it was not the King but Parliament. Parliament had established a Committee of Safety to co-ordinate strategy; moreover during 1643 it set about forming associations of counties to overcome the ingrained localism which caused men to refuse to fight outside their county boundaries unless they were soldiers by trade. This arrangement naturally led to the formation of other Parliamentarian armies beyond that directly under the command of the Earl of Essex. In the west Sir William Waller, who as a young man had fought in the same regiment as Essex at the beginning of the Thirty Years War in Germany and also served as a volunteer in the Venetian army, was appointed by Essex as a Major-General. Waller advanced from Winchester as far as Salisbury and then energetically swept round Dorset and Gloucestershire, seizing Tewkesbury on the River Severn. Waller's 'army' consisted of a mere 1300 men, and in a clash by the Severn with the Royalists under the command of Prince Rupert's younger brother Maurice (Ripple Field, 13 April) he met a check. But Waller remained master of the Severn Valley.

The campaign in the west began early because the winter was mild. Indeed Sir Ralph Hopton, who had also acquired military experience abroad and was to be Waller's principal opponent, had won a victory for the Royalists at Braddock Down near Liskeard in Cornwall as early as 19 January. After that he persuaded the Cornishmen to march into Devon. This was followed by a truce between Cornwall and Devon, which reflected the localized character of the fighting. Meanwhile up in Yorkshire Sir Thomas Fairfax, another soldier of experience, captured Leeds for Parliament. But his force was outnumbered by that of the Earl of Newcastle. Consequently he was only able to control the West Riding. When the Queen returned from her mission to Holland she was able to land at Bridlington in the East Riding and later to join the Earl of Newcastle at York, where she stayed for three months before she made off towards Oxford to meet her husband. To skirt East Anglia (largely under parliamentary control) she went through Pontefract, Newark, Lichfield and Warwickshire. The King dispatched Prince Rupert who, using gunpowder for mining for the first time in England, captured Lichfield Cathedral, fortified and held by the Parliamentarians, on 21 April, and thus prepared the way for the Queen. While

DELINEATIO ABITVS MAGNA BRITTANNIÆ REGINÆ EX HOLLANDIÂ IN ANGLIAM, CVM 29 IAN: AN: 1643 SCHEVENINGÂ SOLVERE

Queen Henrietta Maria, who had been in Holland raising money and collecting arms for the King, landed at Bridlington on 22 February 1643. She had been kept at sea for nine days by violent storms, but remained undaunted by the elements, as is well illustrated by her reported comment to her terrified attendants: 'Comfort yourselves, my dears, Queens of England are never drowned.'

Henrietta Maria was in Yorkshire the Earl of Newcastle had made considerable progress against Fairfax in the West Riding and had indeed succeeded in confining the Yorkshire Parliamentarians largely to the city of Hull, which twice refused to surrender. By the beginning of July the Queen, describing herself as 'Her she-majesty, generalissima', arrived in Newark with an army of her own, and after vainly trying to capture Lincoln, eventually joined the King at Edgehill on 13 July.

Before the Queen's return the two main armies had been confronting each other in the Oxford area. The Earl of Essex, advancing from Windsor with a sizeable army, laid siege to Reading on the road to Oxford. King Charles marched from Oxford to its relief, but before he arrived the town had surrendered. The commander at Reading was court-martialled and condemned to death, but reprieved after an appeal to his father from the thirteen-year-old Prince of Wales (the future Charles II). In a somewhat leisurely way Essex moved from Reading to Thame (thirteen miles south-east of Oxford) preparatory to an attack on Oxford's defences. But Prince Rupert, after his return from his successful mission to Lichfield, crossed the Thames with an expeditionary force to surprise and outmanoeuvre Essex, whose troops still lay scattered. Near Thame Rupert engaged in a skirmish against its reinforced garrison (Chalgrove Field, 18 June) where Colonel John Hampden, the hero of the ship-money case and a close friend of John Pym, was mortally wounded. Essex then abandoned his attempt to blockade Oxford, while Rupert and his soldiers harried villages round the Chiltern Hills and unnerved the Londoners. On 26 June Essex gloomily volunteered to resign his command, but the offer was not accepted.

Elsewhere throughout the country in June and July the Royalists were equally successful. In Yorkshire Fairfax tried hard to secure the West Riding. He took and then abandoned Wakefield; on 30 June he faced a superior army commanded by the Earl of Newcastle on Adwalton Moor near Bradford, where he was severely defeated. Fairfax and his father, who, being a peer, was in nominal command, then decided to withdraw from the West Riding; Sir Thomas Fairfax brought the remnants of his exhausted cavalry to Hull where, through the courtesy of the Earl of Newcastle, he was joined by his formidable wife, a de Vere.

Meanwhile in the west of England Hopton had won a series of victories for the King. His success at the battle of Stratton in north-west Cornwall was astonishing; for he inflicted a defeat on the Parliamentarians under the Earl of Stamford, with a force outnumbered by two to one and short of munitions and food, chiefly through

Samuel Cooper, a miniaturist of genius, described by Samuel Pepys as 'a great painter', produced studies of several Parliamentarian leaders. Among them was this unfinished watercolour miniature of Oliver Cromwell, held by many to be the finest likeness of the Lord Protector

Prince Rupert of the Rhine (1619–82), the nephew of Charles I, who appointed him
captain-general in 1644, is portrayed here in a work attributed to Gerrit Van Honthorst.
He was a brilliant cavalry commander, but as a young officer over-exuberant. Later he
served Charles II as an admiral of ability

CHARLES R. CHARLES P.

RUSTY and well-beloved We greet you well. Whereas We have received information that those Souldiers which have been forward to serve Us in the Forlorn hope, are not looked upon according to their merited Valour and Loyall service. We doe therefore require, that from hence-forward the Commanders in chiefe, both of Horse and Foot, which lead up the Forlorne-hope, upon whom also We mean to bestow speciall tokens of Our Princely favour, doe signify in writing the names of those souldiers whom they find most forward in serving Us their King, and Country, that care may be taken to reward their deservings, and make them specially known to all Our good Subjects; For which end we have thought fit to require Sir *William Parkhurst*, Knight, and *Thomas Bushell*, Esquire, Wardens of Our Mint, to provide from time to time certain Badges of Silver, containing Our Royall Image, and that of Our dearest sonne Prince *Charles*, to be delivered to weare on the breast of every man who shall be certified under the hands of their Commanders in chiefe to have done us faithfull service in the Forlorne-hope. And we doe therefore most straitly command, That no Souldier at any time doe sell, nor any of Our Subjects presume to buy or weare any of these said Badges, other then they, to whom we shall give the same, and that under such paine and punishment as Our Councell of Warre shall think fit to inflict, if any shall presume to offend against this Our Royall command. And We farther require the said Commanders, and Wardens of Our Mint, to keep severall Registers of the names of those, and of their Country, for whom they shall give their Certificates. *Given at Our Court at* OXFORD, *the Eighteenth day of* May. 1643.

To Our Trusty and wellbeloved Sir WILLIAM PARKHURST *Knight, and* THOMAS BUSHELL *Esquire, Wardens of Our Mint at* Oxford

Proclamation of the 'Forlorn Hope Medal', presented to soldiers loyal to the King at Oxford in May 1643 the courage of his infantry. Hopton again advanced into Devon, from which Stamford drove him out, and thence into Gloucestershire. On 5 July Hopton faced his old friend, Waller, at Lansdown, north of Bath, and again through the heroism of the Cornish infantry defeated him in a bloody battle. Eight days later the two armies met again on Roundway Down. The Royalists were exhausted after their supreme effort at Lansdown; Hopton himself had been wounded by a gunpowder explosion and could play little part. But after the battle he brought off his men safely to Devizes in Wiltshire. Thence Prince Maurice, who was serving with Hopton, rode off to Oxford in search of reinforcements. In response to this appeal Prince Rupert himself arrived with fourteen regiments to join the western army. Together they laid siege to Bristol which they surrounded and assaulted on 26 July. After fierce fighting during which a breach was effected to the north-west of the city (at Frome Gate), the Governor surrendered. The capture of Bristol, the second most valuable port in the country, was a moment of supreme triumph for the Royalist cause. Even in eastern England where the Parliamentarians were relatively powerful they suffered rebuffs. Though the cavalry regiment raised by Colonel Oliver Cromwell distinguished itself in a skirmish at Gainsborough in Lincolnshire, the Earl of Newcastle's army advanced to the rescue from Yorkshire, and Gainsborough, Lincoln and Stamford were all abandoned to the Royalists by the first week of August.

It would appear that the time had arrived for the implementation of the King's 'grand strategy', had it ever existed, that is to say converging advances upon London. On the contrary it was resolved at Oxford, against the advice of Rupert, to send the main army to capture the city of Gloucester. With Gloucester and Bristol in Royalist hands, communication between Oxford and Wales would be fully opened – a desirable position, for it was in Wales that the population was most loyal to the King. Parliament had been distressed by the series of setbacks everywhere except in East Anglia, where Oliver Cromwell was winning his reputation as a commander and had linked up with Fairfax who was later to become his superior officer; the extremists blamed the Earl of Essex for these failures and wanted William Waller to take over the command. John Pym laboured for a compromise. He managed to reconcile Essex and Waller, who did not love one another; and a new army was raised,

Sir Thomas Fairfax, later Baron Fairfax (1612–71), earned the nickname 'Black Tom'. In the early years of the war, when parliamentary fortunes were at a low ebb, only he and Cromwell seemed immune from defeat. He had supreme command of the New Model Army from its creation in 1645 until 1650, and won the praise of Milton in a famous sonnet: 'Fairfax! whose name in arms through Europe rings . . . Thy firm unshaken virtue ever brings Victory home . . . .'. The names around the illustrations are those of Parliamentarian officers under his charge principally in the City of London, to serve under Waller in the west. In the east an Eastern Association army under the Earl of Manchester was also virtually independent of Essex. At the same time negotiations continued between the English Parliament and leading Scots for a military alliance. An approach had reached Westminster from the Marquis of Argyll, a saturnine and extremely pious Presbyterian, who feared lest Scotland might be invaded by the Irish and the northern English Royalists. Pym sent a deputation to Edinburgh, led by Sir Henry Vane, who had been highly critical of the Earl of Essex and who, not being himself a Presbyterian, was likely to protect the independence of other English Puritans.

The King arrived at Gloucester on 10 August. He set about a formal siege with cannon and attempts at mining. Prince Rupert's advice to take the town by assault, as at Bristol, was rejected on the ground that it would be too costly in human lives. But the young Governor, Edward Massey, defiantly resisted and managed to re-victual the city. Rescue was put in hand at Westminster. The army under the Earl of Essex was reinforced by six regiments of the London trained bands with enough bread, cheese and beer to last it a week. On 5 September the Parliamentarian army reached the Severn and fired a salute to notify Massey that a relieving force had arrived. Regretfully the King withdrew his army, but Rupert was determined to bar Essex's way back to London, aiming to win the war for his side by a big battle.

For nearly a fortnight Essex managed to avoid contact with the Royalist army. Instead of returning by the same route on which he came (via Aylesbury and Stow-on-the-Wold) he moved after a feint into Worcestershire making for Swindon (via Cirencester and Cricklade) and thence Hungerford, Newbury and Reading, all in Berkshire. Rupert's cavalry engaged the left flank of Essex's army (at Aldbourne Chase, north-west of Hungerford) on 18 September, but were driven off. Essex then decided to put the River Kennet, which runs through Newbury, between him and the Royalists; he approached the town of Newbury on 19 September, but two hours earlier Rupert had succeeded in inserting his forces between the Parliamentarians and London. Charles I slept comfortably in New-bury that night after surprising Essex's quartermasters who were arranging billets there. To get home safely Essex now had to fight his

Robert Earle of Essex, his Excellence, Generall of ye Army.

Newbery battell

Peter Stent excudit

Romantic presentations of military commanders, in which past exploits and the men under their command are shown as background, were common. This shows the 3rd Earl of Essex, with the massed pikemen at the battles of Edgehill and Newbury

The area covered by the armies of the King and the Earl of Essex in the weeks which culminated in the first battle of Newbury

way through. He deployed his left wing, over which Major-General Skippon took command, a mile south-west of Newbury while the right wing, which Essex commanded personally, stretched down to a river called the Enbrook, thus guarding against an outflanking movement from the south. The King's army, over-confident, deployed slowly. For some reason or other a body of horse sent to occupy Wash Common plateau on its right centre withdrew before the battle began. Skippon, an old soldier, was also able to seize what was called 'Round Hill' (north of Wash Common) with infantry, thus threatening the south of the Royalist positions. Cannon was mounted on Round Hill where it could command the whole of the plain before Newbury while the Royalist cannon was placed to the east of it. Nevertheless the Earl of Essex is said to have told his soldiers that the enemy had all the advantages, 'the Hill, the Town, Hedges, Lane and River'. Hedges certainly lay between the two lines, but the town of Newbury was Parliamentarian in sympathy while Skippon's infantry held Round Hill.

The Parliamentarians took the offensive, for the Royalists felt they could afford to fight defensively. The battle began at seven o'clock in the morning of 20 September. On both wings the Royalist cavalry was at first victorious. But the infantry in the Parliamentarian centre stood firm. On the left foot soldiers were able to hold up the enemy cavalry in enclosed country, while in the centre Skippon called up his reserves from the London trained bands. There the pikemen aided by cannon-fire on Round Hill, which the Royalists had failed to occupy, finally brought two Royalist cavalry regiments commanded by Sir John Byron to a standstill. Here the contest took place among the hedgerows where the cavalry were at a disadvantage: in trying to penetrate them Lord Falkland, Charles I's Secretary of State and one of the most honourable among the Royalists, was killed; a memorial marks the spot near which he died.

Altogether the battle lasted twelve hours. The King then held a council of war; Rupert and Byron wanted to fight on, but on being informed that the gunpowder was almost exhausted, Charles ordered withdrawal to Oxford. Essex's army got back safely to London by way of Reading on 25 September. According to Lord Clarendon's history, 'The Earl of Essex was received in London with all imaginable demonstrations of affection and reverence, public and solemn thanksgiving was appointed for his victory . . . it may well be reckoned amongst the most soldierly actions of this unhappy war.' A modern military historian has written that the campaign of Gloucester and the first battle of Newbury stamp Essex as one of the greatest commanders of the civil war. It certainly rehabilitated him in the minds of the Parliamentarians after the misadventures during the

The first battle of Newbury

summer. Three years later in an elegy Essex had the credit:

> And you know the gain at Newberry!
> Seeing the General, how undauntedly
> He then encouraged you for England's right!
> When Royal forces fled, he stood the fight!

Essex's victory at the first battle of Newbury was a crucial event in the civil war, though its significance is sometimes glossed over in comparison with the later battles at Marston Moor and Naseby. It is also of interest because though there was flat and open land around Newbury, the fight was concentrated in enclosed country with hedges interspersed by narrow lanes. The size of the two armies was about equal but the Royalists were much stronger in cavalry. In this hilly area of hedges and trees, however, the cavalry was of little value as it was held off by pikemen and, to a lesser extent, by musketeers. It was the only contest in the civil wars (apart from Preston) where the cavalry did not prove to be the queen of the battle. Here too artillery played some part: fifteen-pound and twenty-pound cannon balls have been discovered on the site.

The Parliamentarians, who were in many ways handicapped, being surprised and cut off from their base, fought heroically, the London militiamen in particular distinguishing themselves. The Royalists after their earlier victories may have underestimated their opponents. Yet it was their finest chance to win the war at a blow; for had the army under Essex been destroyed, the capital might have surrendered. As it was, the Parliamentarian triumph at Newbury was a turning-point in the first civil war.

CHAPTER FIVE

The War Widens:
1644

The first battle of Newbury made it clear to both sides that the war was going to last a long time, just as the earlier failure of the negotiations at Oxford, when the King had firmly refused to disband his forces as a preliminary to negotiations, showed that a compromise was impossible. During the last months of his life John Pym (who was to die of cancer in December 1643) used his diplomatic gifts to resume the search for an alliance with the Scots; he also helped to plan the formation of new armies in England which were in effect to be independent of the commander-in-chief. On 7 August commissioners from the Parliament at Westminster had arrived in Leith, including Sir Henry Vane with the Congregational minister Philip Nye as his adviser, and after ten days a Solemn League and Covenant was drawn up comprising the terms for a Christian *entente* between the kingdoms of England and Scotland. The English were seeking military aid, the Scots religious conformity.

The Solemn League and Covenant of 1643 has to be sharply distinguished from the National Covenant embraced earlier by the Scots when they repudiated King Charles I's interference with the Kirk in 1638. By the Solemn League 'noblemen, barons, knights, gentlemen, citizens, burgesses, ministers of the Gospel and commons of all sorts in the kingdoms of England, Scotland and Ireland . . . living under one King and being of the reformed religion' swore to preserve the Church of Scotland and to reform the religion of England and Ireland 'according to the word of God and

The Solemn League and Covenant, accepted at a meeting in St Margaret's Church, Westminster on 25 September 1643, made religious concessions to the Scots in return for their military aid. Its six points, here set out with illustrations in an etching by Hollar, covered the preservation of the Church of Scotland and religious reform in England (I and II); a guarantee to preserve Parliament and the King (III); the punishment of incendiaries and malignants (IV); the preservation of the union of the kingdoms of England, Scotland and Ireland (V); and a pledge to maintain and defend the League (VI)

the example of the best reformed Churches'. The third clause of the League laid it down that they should all 'endeavour with their lives and estates' to protect 'the rights and liberties of parliaments'. The final version of the League was accepted at a meeting in St Margaret's Church, Westminster (then called 'Margaret's' so as not to offend the susceptibilities of the Puritans) on 25 September. It had already been agreed to by-pass the remnants of the House of Lords. Those who swore to the Solemn League included members not only of the House of Commons but also of the Assembly of Divines which had been constituted on 1 July to advise Parliament about religious reforms. Parliament had already abolished bishops and confiscated their lands, but Philip Nye, who was invited to open the proceedings on the grave occasion, was careful to point out that they were not committed to imitate the precise organization of the Scottish Kirk. That proviso was to be the source of future arguments. But Pym had got what he wanted, a military alliance. To pay for the entry of a Scottish army into England a large loan had first to be raised in the City of London, for the English Parliament undertook to pay the entire cost of a Scots army of 21,000 men, which on 19 January 1644 began its march south.

James Graham, Earl of Montrose, a sincere Calvinist who was nevertheless romantically loyal to his King, had warned Queen Henrietta Maria when she was in York and later King Charles when he was outside Gloucester that a Scottish invasion of northern England was imminent. The King was reluctant to believe that the Scots would not remain loyal to him, especially after the conciliatory gestures he had made towards them when he visited Edinburgh in the summer of 1641. But he himself was already seeking help from Ireland. He had ordered his Lord-Lieutenant, the Marquis of Ormonde, to arrange a cessation of hostilities with the rebel Irish, which was concluded on 15 September 1643, in order that English soldiers in the Irish garrison might be brought over to fight on the Royalist side in England. Troops from Munster and Leinster began to arrive in November. Some of them were intended for the defence of Chester (the main staging point from Ireland) and others to reinforce Hopton in the south. When Charles at last recognized the genuineness of the military danger from Scotland, he appointed Montrose, who was an experienced soldier, as his Captain-General

Hillesden House in Buckinghamshire was fortified by Royalist forces in February 1644, and on 4 March Cromwell and Major-General Crawford stormed the house after the garrison refused to surrender. The house itself was razed, and the fifteenth-century north door of its chapel, All Saints', was riddled with bullet holes, almost obliterating the earlier, astronomical decorations there. Montrose held out hopes that with his own kinsmen and servants, and with troops landed on the west coast of Scotland from Ireland, he could distract the Scottish expeditionary army from its rear after it had entered northern England and oblige it to come back home.

In February 1644, a fortnight after Montrose's appointment, a Committee of Both Kingdoms including peers like the Earls of Essex and Warwick, members of parliament like Sir Henry Vane and Oliver Cromwell, and four Scottish representatives was formed to concert the strategy of the war. It was an unwieldy body of twenty-five members, and as its experts were usually away on duty in the field its decisions were not always wise nor realistic. Here the King, as an unchallenged authority, remained at an advantage in the direction of the war from his side. By now the English Parliament had formed two new armies, that of the Eastern Association (Essex, Suffolk, Norfolk, Cambridgeshire, Huntingdonshire and Lincolnshire) under the command of the Earl of Manchester and that of a South-Eastern Association (Sussex, Surrey, Hampshire and Kent) under the able Sir William Waller, which naturally created jealousies. By way of compensation at the beginning of December 1643 a vote was agreed upon to recruit the returned army of the Earl of Essex, bringing it back to a strength of 14,000 men, which was what it had been before the London-trained bands were withdrawn from it after the Newbury campaign.

The course of the war since that battle had favoured neither side. On the one hand, the town of Reading had been abandoned by the Parliamentarians and Prince Maurice had taken the port of Dartmouth in Devon. For a time too Winchester in Hampshire and Arundel in Sussex came under Royalist control. On the other hand, in October the Earl of Essex had taken Newport Pagnell in Buckinghamshire, a strategic point on the route between Yorkshire and London. The Earl of Newcastle was soon obliged to raise the siege of Hull, which he had begun in early September. During the siege Sir Thomas Fairfax – 'Black Tom', as he was called – a taciturn and efficient officer, had brought the cavalry not needed in Hull across the Humber to join up with Manchester's army in Lincolnshire. He and Colonel Cromwell – 'Old Noll' – soon to become Manchester's second-in-command, together defeated the Royalists in

Summoning Hull: a Parliamentarian representation of the King's humiliation, for the second time, before Hull. A Parliamentarian army under Sir Thomas Fairfax made its base at Hull during the second half of 1643. The town was besieged from 2 September until 12 October of that year by Royalist forces under Newcastle, which were eventually withdrawn after an attack upon them by Fairfax's father Ferdinando, Lord Fairfax. At one point during the siege Cromwell entered the town by crossing the Humber from Lincolnshire and helped to evacuate Fairfax's cavalry

a cavalry fight at Winceby on 11 October. As a consequence Lincoln was regained for Parliament. Finally Fairfax, in an inspired march across England in mid-winter, confronted a Royalist force besieging Nantwich, the last Parliamentarian stronghold in Cheshire, which he defeated though the Royalist commander, Lord Byron, had been reinforced by regiments from Ireland (25 January 1644). Among the many prisoners taken was Colonel George Monck, a professional soldier who had seen Charles I and offered him his services as a volunteer, having himself recently returned from a command in Ireland. Fairfax then sat down to reduce the last Royalist stronghold in Lancashire, Lathom House, whose defence was conducted by a middle-aged Frenchwoman, the Countess of Derby.

Thus by the spring of 1644 when hostilities were resumed in earnest England was divided from the military point of view almost equally between the Roundheads, as the Parliamentarians were inappropriately nicknamed (most of the officers were gentlemen who wore their hair long), and the Cavaliers, neither side having been able materially to push back their lines. For example, the Parliamentarians under Waller retook Arundel in Sussex and repulsed the Royalists at the battle of Cheriton in Hampshire (29 March), but in Nottingham-shire they were still frustrated in their efforts to occupy the key town of Newark, which was relieved by Prince Rupert on 21 March. The arrival of the Scottish army altered the whole situation. The Earl of Newcastle ceased to have a firm hold on north-eastern England. By 20 April the Scots had safely linked up with Fairfax, returned from his successful mission to Cheshire and Lancashire, and together they laid siege to the ancient northern capital of York.

The entry of the large Scottish army into Northumberland left the Marquis of Newcastle, as he now was, with no alternative but to reinforce the garrison of the town from which he had taken his title and then, adopting delaying tactics, fall back slowly through County Durham to his stronghold at York. But in April his difficulties were increased when Sir Thomas Fairfax, flushed with his victory at Nantwich, returned to the West Riding of Yorkshire and joined his father, who came from Hull to meet him, at Selby. Learning that the Fairfaxes were preparing to meet up with the Scots near Durham, Lord Bellasis, the temporary commander at York, bravely set out to prevent this, but was comprehensively defeated by Thomas Fairfax (who was his cousin), losing all his officers and 2,000 of his men. When Newcastle learned of the disaster, he gave up his intention of confronting the Scots at Durham and hastened to shut himself up in York where he had some 4,500 infantry and 3,000 cavalry. While Fairfax, now in command of almost the whole of Yorkshire, was meeting Alexander Leslie, Earl of Leven, the commander-in-chief of the Scots army, Newcastle wrote to the King in alarm, saying that the enemy 'have already put themselves in such a posture as will soon ruin us, being at York unless there is some speedy course taken to give us relief'.

The situation was, however, not one of immediate danger. York was a strongly fortified city with thick stone walls three and a half miles in circumference which dated back to the Middle Ages. It contained an inner and outer moat and was protected by half a dozen gun emplacements on small forts. Supplies of food and munitions were sufficient to last the garrison for some weeks; on 22 April

Newcastle decided to let most of his cavalry depart to join the King
in the Midlands; he kept only 300 horse in the city. Thus the strain
on his supplies was considerably diminished.

Although the Scots and the army of the Fairfaxes took up siege
positions the day before, these were too few to carry out a complete
blockade; so for some time Newcastle was able to send out foraging
parties into the area north of the city. The consequence was that
Fairfax decided to ride over to the Earl of Manchester, whose army
had captured Lincoln on 6 May (the town had changed hands more
than once) to invite him to take part in the siege. Manchester
accepted the invitation and reached York in a leisurely way during
the first week of June. The three besieging armies were now able
more or less to complete the encirclement and investment of the city.
Manchester's troops covered the north, the Scots the west and the
south, and Fairfax the east. To link up his forces with those of the
Scots to his west Manchester had a bridge of boats constructed across
the River Ouse at the suburb of Poppleton. What the three
commanders had in mind was to starve the city into surrender if it
could not be taken by direct assault. The artillery of those days was
insufficiently powerful seriously to breach the thick walls; the only
hope was mining. Cavalry patrolled the suburbs to prevent forays by
the garrison. Both sides cannonaded each other from time to time
without doing much damage. The Marquis of Newcastle had no
intention of surrendering easily; he trusted the King to send a
relieving force; meanwhile he was content to offer to treat with the
enemy in the hope of gaining time.

After the parleys ended without result, the most dramatic event in
the siege took place. Since Manchester's arrival while the city had
been closely beleaguered tunnels had been built from the northern
side with the aim of springing two mines, one under one of the city
gates, the other under one of the four towers of St Mary's Manor, a
large house which had been the headquarters of the Lord President of
the North in the days of the rule of Viscount Strafford. The mine
under St Mary's was exploded on the morning of Trinity Sunday
(16 June) apparently by the order of Major-General Lawrence Crawford, who commanded the infantry in the army of the Earl of
Manchester (Oliver Cromwell commanded the cavalry). Whether
Manchester knew of his subordinate's intention or not is obscure. But

The Earl of Newcastle was held in awe by his soldiers and his enemies alike. Here he is represented accepting the genuflexion of his horses

what is certain is that neither of the other generals was informed of the plan. No doubt the Presbyterian Crawford thought it an excellent time to assault the city while many of the officers of the garrison were attending Anglican service in the Cathedral. The tower or part of it was duly blown up and a battery breached a hole in the wall near by. Crawford gallantly led his men into the breach, aiming to take the manor-house by storm, but many of the garrison troops were able to concentrate against him and he lost 300 out of 600 of his soldiers. It was suggested afterwards that if the other generals had been notified about the attempt they could have created diversions. As it was, the besiegers were dispirited, illness was rife among the soldiers, and

96

Compton-Wynyates in Warwickshire was built by Sir William Compton in the early
sixteenth century, incorporating sections of an earlier moated hall which stood on the
site. Staunch Royalists, the Comptons garrisoned soldiers in a barrack-room which
survives to this day. The house was captured in June 1644 by the Parliamentarian
Colonel Purefoy and was used until the end of the war as a parliamentary base

rumours that Prince Rupert was on his way with a big army
produced, apart from a sally or two, a fortnight of inaction.

Meanwhile what had been happening elsewhere? The Parliamentarians had made an all-out effort at the outset of the 1644 campaign.
Besides the Scots, they had four armies in the field. The original
intention had been that the armies of the Earl of Essex and Sir
William Waller should meet at Aylesbury in Buckinghamshire and
move against the King's base at Oxford. Eventually they met at
Reading (which the Royalists in turn had abandoned) in the middle
of May. By the end of the month Essex had occupied first Abingdon
and then Islip, both close to Oxford, while Waller aimed to cut off
the King from his adherents in the west. Charles I was obliged by

this pressure to move out of Oxford into Worcestershire, having
allowed Prince Rupert with the bulk of his forces to go north to the
rescue of York. But the trouble was that the two Parliamentarian
generals, as has been noted, did not get along happily together. Essex
was jealous of Waller, who was probably the more capable of the two.
He therefore decided to leave Waller to shadow the King, while he
himself marched to the west of England. His immediate objective
was to relieve the port of Lyme in Dorset, which was being besieged
by Prince Maurice with a small force; Essex's argument was that if he
could crush Royalism in the south-west of England, he would
deprive the King of his principal source of supplies and thus shorten
the war. He was also afraid that Lord Hopton would join Prince
Maurice and recruit an entirely new western army for the Royalist
side. The Committee of Both Kingdoms was dismayed by the
decision to break up the combined army, which was intended to
overthrow the King, and thus cease to be a threat to Oxford. But
what could the Committee do? Most of the members were civilians,
for officers like Manchester and Cromwell were engaged elsewhere. If
the commander-in-chief chose to advance into the west, who were
they to gainsay his considered judgment? The Earl of Essex adopted
the attitude that earlier directives had instructed him to relieve Lyme
and that it was his responsibility to give orders to his own
Major-General, that is to say Waller. Essex also took care not to
inform the Committee of his intentions until he was well on his way
in the middle of June. Waller, left to deal with the King, was
defeated at the battle of Cropredy Bridge. Cropredy Bridge lay across
the River Cherwell not far from Banbury. The two forces (each
consisting of about 9,000 men, although Waller had more infantry)
had been moving north in parallel lines on either side of the river.
The King's army was strung out in three bodies. Waller, who had
seized the bridge, thrust two contingents across the river, one over
the bridge, another at a ford a mile farther south, but they were
separately defeated and when his infantry tried to hold the ford,
because they were pikemen – their musketeers having separated from
them – they were mown down and fled. Waller withdrew his small
army to higher ground west of the Cherwell where the Royalists
could scarcely hope to attack them effectively. Instead of an attack he
received an engaging letter from a Royalist lady who had formerly

been a flame of his, suggesting that he should change sides; but Waller remained true to his cause and drew off his men without further serious mishap. Casualties had been slight on either side, but Waller admitted that he had been worried by his loss of eleven guns and he left Charles at liberty to return to Oxford or to follow Essex into the west of England. The King for his part distinguished himself in this minor action.

Thus although the Royalists were outnumbered, they were not yet outmanoeuvred. For they still enjoyed the advantage of inner lines; the Parliamentarians were never sure where they would strike next. Indeed when Rupert was in Oxford early in May he had advised his master to reduce his commitments in the Oxford area by securing a number of strong points including Reading and Banbury while the King himself kept a cavalry force (in later days it would be called an army of manoeuvre) which could go to the assistance of any threatened garrison. By that means Rupert himself would be left free to advance north with a sizeable Royalist army. His plan was accepted, but after Rupert left Oxford on 5 May the King, apparently on the advice of the old professional, Lord Forth, now created Earl of Brentford, who was slow, gouty and deaf, reduced his commitments even further by abandoning Reading once again and embodying its garrison in his own army. As it proved, the decision worked out excellently, partly because the Earl of Essex had left Waller too small a force to incommode the King, who was thus left free, like Rupert, to go wherever he wished.

After Rupert left Oxford he first made for Lancashire to recruit his strength in an area largely Royalist in sympathy. In the space of a fortnight he moved through Stockport in Cheshire and Bolton, Wigan, Liverpool and Preston in Lancashire, relieving on his way Lathom House, still indomitably held by the Countess of Derby against the parliamentary besiegers left behind by Fairfax. The Committee of Both Kingdoms was sufficiently perturbed to send Sir Henry Vane to York to urge the generals there to dispatch an expedition into Lancashire so as to regain Fairfax's earlier conquests. Though the evidence is rather flimsy, it has been thought – and this is seemingly accepted by his latest biographer – that Vane also wanted to sound the three generals besieging York about the idea that the King, once he was beaten, should be deposed and a republic

The indomitable Frenchwoman Charlotte de la Trémoille, Countess of Derby (1599–
1664), who twice conducted the defence of Lathom House, Lancashire, against
Parliamentarian forces. In the spring of 1644 after four months of siege she was relieved
by Prince Rupert but, a year later, in December 1645, she was compelled to surrender
after another long siege under the direction of Thomas Fairfax

established in place of the monarchy. But the generals could not be persuaded to divide or divert their armies; they took the view that Rupert would sooner or later come their way and that they then could deal with him. They were right.

On 14 June Charles I had written a letter to Rupert in which he peremptorily commanded him to march at once to the relief of York, saying 'If York be lost, I shall esteem my crown little less . . .'. A succession of historians and biographers have written glosses on this letter, which is obscurely worded. Rupert certainly interpreted it to mean that not only was he to relieve York but to 'beat the rebels' armies which were before it'. A modern military historian has averred that no staff officer today could have thought that Charles intended his nephew to fight a battle at all costs whether the siege of York had been raised or not. Yet at the time John Culpeper, the King's Chancellor of the Exchequer, observed to Charles after the letter was dispatched, 'Before God, you are undone, for upon the peremptory order, he will fight whatever comes on't.'

The commanders round York learned on 28 June that Rupert was on his way; two days later he was known to be in Knaresborough, which lies about twelve miles west of York. A council of war was held and it was decided to march out to meet him, for the generals had no wish to be caught between Rupert's relieving army and the garrison under Newcastle sallying forth from the city (in the same way and for the same reason that King Charles had resolved to raise the siege of Gloucester the year before). They therefore led their armies on to Marston Moor, four miles west of York, so as to bar any approach from Knaresborough. Their cavalry was sent ahead and the infantry followed. They could not imagine that Rupert would advance upon York in any other way, for then he would be obliged to follow a circuitous route crossing first the River Ouse, then its tributary the Swale and finally the Ouse again at Poppleton where the bridge of boats had been left in charge of a regiment of dragoons. The Prince, however, did precisely that. On 1 July his infantry made a forced march of twenty-two miles from Knaresborough by way of Boroughbridge to the north and then turned west along the west side of the river Ouse, surprised the dragoons, captured the bridge of boats, and encamped his foot soldiers and artillery in the forest of Galtres north of York.

After he himself arrived in York that evening Prince Rupert held a meeting with the Marquis of Newcastle, who had greeted his raising of the siege with 'nothing but thankfulness and obedience', and James King Lord Eythin, a professional soldier, who was the Marquis's General of Foot. Neither Newcastle nor Eythin was anxious to fight the three allied armies, which together obviously outnumbered Rupert's even when it was reinforced by the York garrison; they wanted to await reinforcements from farther north and hoped that the allies, demoralized by the relief of York, would quarrel among themselves. But Rupert insisted that he had positive orders from King Charles to fight a battle. Newcastle said he was prepared to obey the Prince in all things. Rupert then explained that he wanted all the Royalist forces to be ready to march out to meet the enemy at 4 a.m. on the following morning.

While Rupert was leading his infantry towards York he had detached a strong force of cavalry to confront the allied armies ranged on Marston Moor. The allied commander at first assumed that Rupert's whole army was on its way there and that a battle was imminent on 1 July. However when no infantry appeared and the Royalist cavalry, having faced them a while, wheeled back out of sight, they decided to move south-west towards Leeds via Tadcaster. Exactly why they resolved to do so is by no means clear: according to two different Parliamentarian accounts their object was to prevent the Prince from marching south either to rejoin the King or to invade the territory of the Eastern Association south of Newark, left vulnerable in the absence of the Earl of Manchester's army. They had gone some distance along the road to Tadcaster when Lieutenant-General Thomas Fairfax, commanding the Yorkshire cavalry, which had been left to guard the rear, reported that the Royalist cavalry had reappeared on Marston Moor and urged his superiors (he was supported in his appeal by Lieutenant-General Cromwell and Major-General David Leslie) to recall the infantry from the Tadcaster area and 'make a stand'; for otherwise the danger was that the Royalists would attack them while 'in column of march' so that they would be put 'in risk of destruction in a running fight'. Acting on this advice, around nine o'clock on the morning of 2 July the whole allied armies were ordered by the Earl of Leven to return towards York. They spent the rest of the morning and early afternoon drawing up in order of

Having initially offered his services to King Charles I and been captured during the siege of Nantwich and imprisoned in the Tower of London, George Monck later fought for Parliament against the rebels in Ireland. After the King's execution he served under Cromwell in Scotland

Deployment of the armies at the battle of Marston Moor

battle on the sloping land covered with rye known as Marston Field, facing the moor from the south.

Meanwhile Prince Rupert had led the rest of his army out of York across the Ouse and began deploying his cavalry, infantry and artillery upon Marston Moor. The Marquis of Newcastle, accompanied by his life-guard, joined Rupert there on the morning of 2 July, as arranged, but told the Prince that Lord Eythin would not arrive with the York garrison until the afternoon. Eythin did not reach the moor until about four o'clock. Whether because he did not want to engage in a battle he deliberately procrastinated is not certain. At any rate Rupert decided that it was too late for him to attack the enemy that day; he therefore drew up his troops in a defensive position. He stationed musketeers along a ditch backed by a hedge which lay (though not continuously) between the two armies and gave orders to Lord Byron, who was put in command on the right wing, not to advance if attacked but to wait to fight until the cavalry opposed to him had negotiated the various obstacles in front of them, which included, besides the ditch, a warren and a swamp, and had been disorganized by the fire of the musketeers. The layout of the Royalist left wing under the command of Lord Goring was somewhat similar except that the allied infantry opposed to him, led by Sir Thomas Fairfax, would be obliged to attack him along a narrow lane with a ditch on one side and a hedge on the other, both lined by Royalist musketeers.

The allied left wing opposite Lord Byron was under the orders of Lieutenant-General Oliver Cromwell, who early that day secured the occupation of a hillock and a rabbit warren to the left of his line, thus ensuring that his troops could not be outflanked, and later he brought up two field guns to knock out a small enemy battery which had been placed in support of the Royalist right wing. Cromwell's cavalry was deployed in three lines along a ridge: this enabled his troopers to charge downhill on to the moor.

Between the two cavalry wings the infantry on both sides were drawn up in the centre of the battlefield. The allied foot soldiers from all three armies, the Scots, the Eastern Association army under the Earl of Manchester, and the Yorkshiremen under Lord Fairfax, consisted of fourteen brigades or about 14,000 men; the Royalist infantry amounted to some 10,000 men. The two armies were aligned unusually close together: consequently the casualties were to be heavy. When Lord Eythin eventually arrived and Rupert showed him the disposition of his regiments Eythin said rudely: 'By God, sir, it is very fine in the paper, but there is no such thing in the field.' By this he may have meant that the Royalist forces were marshalled too close to the enemy for safety or possibly that because Rupert had assumed that the infantry from York would have arrived earlier he had placed them at a point where the Royalist centre was in fact too thinly spread. At any rate it was impossible to alter the dispositions so late in the day.

During the afternoon nothing much happened except for a cannonade by both sides. Because of the late arrival of Newcastle's foot soldiers Rupert determined that the Royalists could not take the offensive until the following morning. The Marquis of Newcastle asked Rupert if he was sure that the enemy might not attack them sooner. The Prince answered that they would not do so. Evidently he was convinced that in any case his defensive arrangements were sufficient to prevent this. Indeed as evening drew on and little occurred except a crash of thunder and the fall of summer rain the Cavalier generals felt satisfied the battle would not begin until the next day.

However the allied commander-in-chief, the little old soldier, the Scots Earl of Leven, had other ideas. A summer's night, he declared, was as long as a winter's day. It may well be that the Scots General had ordered a reconnaissance before Newcastle's infantry, known as the Whitecoats after the undyed woollen uniforms they wore, arrived from York and was sure that his three armies vastly outnumbered the Royalists. In fact they did so by perhaps as much as 7,500 men, although the disparity in the cavalry was relatively small – about 6,500 against 8,000 – while the Scots brigades were poorly mounted. Since the cavalry was to determine the course of the battle this was very important. After the battle of Edgehill Rupert had reason to believe that his cavalrymen excelled in quality. So he was hardly being foolish when he courted battle. Nevertheless it was the Earl of Leven who, wisely as it turned out, ordered the offensive that summer evening.

On both wings the cavalry faced one another; and in both cases platoons of musketeers were interspersed, after the Swedish fashion, with the troops of mounted men. The Royalists were taken completely by surprise when the signal to attack was given by a road of cannon on Marston Field about seven in the evening: the battle was all over two hours later when bright moonlight still permitted pursuit by the victors.

The battle began when Cromwell's men charged on the left wing of the field. 'We came down,' recounted his Scoutmaster-General, Lionel Watson, 'in the bravest order and with the greatest resolution that ever was seen . . . In a moment we were past the ditch into the Moor, upon equal grounds with the enemy, our men into a running march.' After Lord Byron's first line, charging (understandably enough) against Prince Rupert's orders, had suffered defeat in a counter-attack, his second line, commanded by Lord Molyneux, a Roman Catholic nobleman from Lancashire, put up the fiercest resistance. Rupert, who was enjoying his supper when the battle began, summoned possibly by Molyneux, mounted his horse and galloped over to his right wing to lead his own cavalry regiment to the rescue, but was unable except momentarily to check his enemy's offensive.

Major-General David Leslie, who with a small force of cavalry was in command of Cromwell's third line, attacked Lord Molyneux's brigade from the flank and soon the Royalist right wing was completely routed. Cromwell received a slight wound in his neck, but did not have to leave the field to have it dressed. He soon returned to the scene of the action to rally and steady his troopers.

Meanwhile the Royalist left wing, consisting of battle-hardened northern cavalry interspersed with musketeers under Lord Goring's command, had defeated the allied cavalry on the right, led by Sir Thomas Fairfax, who confessed that 'by reason of the whins [furze] and ditches which we were to pass over before we could get to the enemy . . . put us in great disorder'. Fairfax's younger brother was mortally wounded and Sir Thomas himself, removing the white paper which signified his allegiance from his helmet, thus enabling him to be mistaken for one of the Royalist officers, succeeded in crossing the battlefield to the left wing in a desperate effort to obtain help. Whether he met Cromwell is uncertain. At any rate Oliver learned of the disaster to his allies on the right after his own success on the left; thereupon he led his cavalry across the centre of the field,

S^R WILLIAM WALLER *Knight Sargeant*
Maiar Generall, of y^e *Parliaments army, and*
a member, of y^e *Hono*^{ble} *House of Commons.*

C.J. *pinxit*   I 6-4-3   *Rodttermondt incidit*
Pieter Stent Excudit

Sir William Waller, glorified here at the height of his success in 1643 supported by some of the infantry belonging to the Earl of Manchester's army, to confront the triumphant General Goring. Goring's men were now scattered and were busy rifling Fairfax's baggage train. Through the smoke and dust Goring perceived that Cromwell's cavalry, outnumbering his own, were advancing along the lane where he had earlier defeated Fairfax. As Cromwell's Scoutmaster wrote, 'the enemy seeing us come in such a gallant posture to charge them, left all thought of pursuit, and began to think that they must fight again, for that victory which they had already got,' while Sir Hugh Cholmeley, the Governor of Scarborough, who heard an account of the battle from the Marquis of Newcastle, thought that 'if Goring's men had been kept close together as did Cromwell's and not dispersed themselves in pursuit, in all probability it had come to a drawn battle at worst'.

After Cromwell's troopers had thus reversed the fortunes on the right wing by defeating Goring's cavalry, they next attacked the Royalist infantry. The discipline and endurance of Cromwell's men was astonishing. The Royalist infantry had been supported by two cavalry regiments stationed in position by Rupert. The Marquis of Newcastle was in charge there and a furious onslaught by his infantry regiments had driven back many of the Scottish and East Anglian foot soldiers in a state of panic. Thinking they had been defeated the two senior generals, the Earl of Leven and Sir Thomas Fairfax's father, Lord Fairfax, actually fled from the field. But the Scottish pikemen rallied and Cromwell's weary troopers arrived to the rescue. Only one Royalist infantry regiment, known as Newcastle's 'Lambs', resisted courageously to the end. First they 'peppered' the Eastern Association cavalry 'soundly with their shot' and then 'stoutly bore them up with their pikes'. In the end they died with their boots on, headed by their colonel.

Some modern military historians have tried to make out that it was not Oliver Cromwell who was chiefly responsible for the Roundhead victory at Marston Moor: it has been ascribed to Sir Thomas Fairfax, to David Leslie as Oliver's second-in-command, or even to Major-General Lawrence Crawford from whom, it is claimed, Oliver 'pitifully' asked for advice. Crawford was in charge of the Scots foot on the left of the centre. But it is highly unlikely that he took over the command of the cavalry from Major-General Leslie while

Plymouth was resolutely Parliamentarian and twice held off attack by the Royalist armies, in 1643 and 1644. This map shows the line of triangular forts built some distance north of the old walls. However, without control of the sea the town would have been all but defenceless

Cromwell was having his wound dressed. Scoutmaster-General Watson's account of the battle, which is the most detailed from the Roundhead side, mentions Cromwell's slight wound, but does not say he left the field and attributes the glorious victory (after God) to the Earl of Manchester's horse and foot led on by Cromwell, while in the most recent assessment of the battle the author has written 'it is certain that Cromwell need share the honour of the Allied victory with no one'. Even if the part played by Oliver is minimized, the fact remains that it was the thorough way in which he had trained his cavalry – so much better disciplined than Rupert's – that turned the

The civil war provided dramatic subject matter for nineteenth-century artists such as John Frederick Herring (1795–1865). This painting conjures up an image of a troop of Roundhead cavalry at a ford

John Frederick Herring the younger (1815–1907) also chose to portray events in the civil war. In this detail from one of his works on the period, our attention is focused on a cavalry skirmish

Semi-derelict by the seventeenth century, Restormel Castle was nonetheless garrisoned in August 1644 as an outpost of the Parliamentarian base at Lostwithiel. It was captured by Royalist troops on 21 August scale. As for Rupert's role, he had some brilliant tactical ideas, but the mistakes he committed were those of an overconfident and enthusiastic young commander. At any rate he survived to rally his shattered army and lived to fight another day, whereas the Marquis of Newcastle, the personal friend of King Charles I and the governor of his son, could not stomach the disgrace of the defeat and left England to go into exile abroad.

The Earl of Essex had experienced no difficulty in relieving Lyme in the middle of June. On 10 July the Parliamentarians occupied Taunton in Somerset and on 23 July Essex also relieved Plymouth in

At the beginning of the war Newcastle, along with the other busy ports of Portsmouth and Chester, was under Royalist control. Newcastle finally fell to the Scots army hired by the Parliamentarians on 19 October 1644. Since York was also lost by the Royalists in that year, this left them with virtually no base in the north-east of the country

Devon. Next he crossed the River Tamar into Cornwall in pursuit of his intention to win the whole of the south-west from the King. But by then Charles himself was on Essex's heels. Essex occupied Lostwithiel, a port on the River Fowey, in order to maintain contact with the Earl of Warwick and the Parliamentarian fleet. The traditional loyalty of the Cornish people was aroused by the coming of the King, who was careful not to impound supplies and prohibited acts of violence by his soldiers. By the end of the first week in August the Royalists began to corner the army of Essex. There were in fact four Royalist armies in Devon (though the whole of them barely equalled a modern division). When Prince Maurice and Lord Hopton joined the King and Sir Richard Grenville arrived from the abandoned siege of Plymouth, the King had collected 16,000 men against 10,000 Parliamentarians, Essex having dispersed some of his troops on garrison duties. On 7 August Charles called upon Essex to surrender. When he refused, his force was methodically hemmed into a narrow strip of land stretching from Lostwithiel to the harbour of Fowey village, the Royalists taking command of the hills that dominated it and thus threatening their enemy's access to the sea. On 31 August Sir William Balfour and 2,000 Parliamentarian cavalry successfully cut their way out, escaped up the Bodmin road and arrived safely in Plymouth. After that Essex threw in the towel. 'I thought it fit', he wrote, 'to look to myself, it being a greater terror to me to be a slave to their contempts than a thousand deaths.' He got away in a fishing-boat but all his infantry surrendered. They were granted extremely lenient terms. Officers were allowed to retain their arms and the soldiers were permitted, once they reached Portsmouth or Southampton, to fight again. It was a curious decision. But the Cornish had had enough of the Parliamentarians' depredations. The beaten foot soldiers were obliged to march without food or shelter on the way; they were stripped of their very clothes. Of the 6,000 men who left Lostwithiel on 2 September only 1,000 survived. The rest died of starvation, disease and exposure. It was one of the most terrible episodes in the first civil war.

After the battle of Marston Moor the three Parliamentarian armies had broken up; the Scots went north to besiege Newcastle upon Tyne which fell to them on 19 October. Manchester's army returned to the Eastern Association and Fairfax to Yorkshire. In the Midlands Waller was still licking his wounds after his defeat at Cropredy Bridge. Thus the House of Commons needed to take the military dispositions into account so as urgently to repair the damage done at Lostwithiel and to prevent the King's return to Oxford. The Earl of Essex was not censured for his misfortune, which he himself blamed on one of his subordinates. Instead Manchester and Waller were instructed to join up with the remnants of Essex's army. Manchester, who was dispirited and anxious to bring the war to an end by negotiation, obeyed his orders slowly and incompletely. But the King was also moving slowly, for his army was tired, unpaid and half-starved after

This engraving depicts the visit of Henrietta Maria to Prince William of Orange at
Nassau in 1644. The Queen had travelled to buy arms from the Prince, who was her
son-in-law, during the first civil war. Later she was strongly opposed to the Duke of
York's remaining in Amsterdam (after his recent escape from London disguised as a girl)
while she and his elder brother, the future Charles II, used Paris as their base in 1648

its long marches and exhausting campaign. It was not until
15 October that he reached Salisbury by way of Chard and Sherborne.
On the 18th he left Salisbury and chased Waller out of Andover. But
Waller got away to meet Manchester at Basingstoke. On 21 October
Essex joined Manchester at Basing House, eight miles south-east of
Newbury, which was reached by the Royalists on 22 October.

The Committee of Both Kingdoms made a pusillanimous decision
about the command of the united armies: it appointed no single
general to command and left it to a council of war to take charge of

operations. On this council Waller was the stalwart. He declared, speaking of the Royalists at Newbury: 'Destroy this [army] and the work is ended.' Manchester was less enthusiastic, while Essex, who had caught a cold, never joined the council of war at all. The united army consisted of 19,000 men of whom 8,000 were cavalry; the King had about 10,000 men and had summoned Prince Rupert to his aid, but the Prince did not arrive until after the ensuing battle.

The second battle of Newbury was fought north of the area covered by the first battle there, and this time the Royalists again faced east. The King's army was ably deployed. The town of Newbury and the River Kennet protected its right flank. In the centre stood a large mansion called Shaw House, which was converted into a formidable strong point. The left rested on the River Lambourne, a tributary of the Kennet, while to the left rear was Donnington Castle, a small fortress which had been held by the Royalists for over a year, and south of it the village of Speen where the reserves under Prince Maurice were placed. The council of war, probably incited by Waller, resolved to divide its forces. The bulk of them were to undertake a fifteen-mile circuitous night march and then attack the enemy at Speen from the rear. Once their objective had been reached Manchester, with the rest of the Parliamentarian army, was to assault Shaw House, where the Royalists would presumably be weakened and distracted. Some military historians have commended the boldness of the plan. But it had its defects: first, it meant dividing the army (the great Duke of Marlborough's last words are said to have been 'Don't divide the army'). Secondly, it was planned and carried out by a committee; even the attack on Speen was in the hands of four different commanders. Thirdly, it involved a long night march, one of the most difficult operations in war. Fourthly, it required cavalry to act in what was largely enclosed country. Lastly, its success depended upon a precise synchronization of attacks, which was extremely hard to achieve in the seventeenth century.

In fact though the night march and the attack were carried out successfully and the village of Speen fell to the Parliamentarians at three o'clock in the afternoon of 27 October, the Royalists, who had received warning of a coming assault on their rear, rallied and drove the enemy back. This check came at five o'clock, by which time it

Map of the second battle of Newbury, 27 October 1644

was dark. The Earl of Manchester did not assault Shaw House with his infantry columns until about four, when he should have begun an hour earlier, and he was repulsed. The losses on both sides were relatively small. The King got away safely and was able to return later with Rupert, whom he had finally appointed as his overall commander in place of the doddery Lord Brentford, to relieve Donnington Castle which contained cannon and valuable stores and which the Parliamentarians had been unable to capture. Manchester had preferred to secure the town of Newbury after the battle rather than to attack Donnington Castle again. A fortnight later Charles I was back in Oxford to take up his winter quarters.

The second battle of Newbury is often described as a victory by the Parliamentarians because they held the field while the King was forced to retire or retreat. But the object of the battle was to prevent the King's return to Oxford, and afterwards, because it was night and the Parliamentarian cavalry was tired, he was not pursued very far.

Furthermore the Parliamentarians were unable even after the departure of the King's army to occupy Donnington Castle. Manchester's slowness in arriving and the lack of energy which he displayed in the battle aroused suspicions. After the battle he replied to a criticism by Sir Arthur Haslerig who fought there: 'Thou art a bloody fellow. God give us peace, for God does never prosper us in our victories to make them clear victories.' The defeat of the Earl of Essex at Lostwithiel and Manchester's failures – both the Earls had disobeyed orders from the Committee of Both Kingdoms – caused Parliament to realize that it must raise fresh armies and find better generals if it was to win the war.

CHAPTER SIX

Parliament's Victory: 1645–1646

The campaign of 1644 ended in an atmosphere of frustration and bitterness on both sides. The King had demoted his principal military advisers and relegated two other leading officers, Lord Wilmot and Lord Percy, whom he replaced with Lord Goring and Lord Hopton, both certainly more capable commanders. Also he had ordered the Governor of Bletchington House near Oxford, which had surrendered to Cromwell, to be put to death for cowardice. On the Parliamentarian side at the beginning of the New Year Sir Alexander Carew, after trial by court martial, was executed for attempting to betray Plymouth to the Royalists, while the House of Commons refused to reprieve the two Hothams, father and son, who having once defied the King, had then planned to hand over the port of Hull to Royalists. On 10 January 1645 Archbishop Laud, the victim of Puritan vindictiveness, after being condemned to death by an Ordinance of Attainder was executed for treason, which he had definitely not committed. As six days before his execution the Book of Common Prayer had been abolished in favour of a Presbyterian directory of worship, this appeared to be the end of an era for the Church of England.

Although the battle of Marston Moor had been won by the Parliamentarians and the cities of York and Newcastle had been lost by the Royalists, thus virtually placing north-east England in the hand of Parliament, these events had to some extent been compensated by the humiliation of Parliament's Lord General at Lostwithiel and by the rebuff suffered by the united Roundhead armies at the second battle of Newbury. Moreover the Marquis of Montrose, Charles I's Captain-General in Scotland, had in August 1644 reached the verge of the Highlands and, raising an army from the clans, occupied Perth and Aberdeen in the King's name. At the beginning of February 1645 he was to defeat the Campbells (the clan of the Marquis of Argyll, the most powerful chieftain in Calvinist Scotland) at the battle of Inverlochy, though Argyll himself only watched it from his barge, moored in a near-by loch, in which he afterwards escaped. The only area where the parliamentary forces had been consistently successful was East Anglia (except for the failure to capture Newark). In 1644 Lincoln had been taken by the Eastern Association army under Edward Montagu, the Earl of Manchester. Moreover Manchester's Lieutenant-General of Horse, Oliver Cromwell, had won his spurs at Marston Moor and was rightly regarded as the moving spirit in military affairs in that part of England.

The Montagus and the Cromwells were both well-established families in Huntingdonshire. They had shared the representation of the county or county town in the House of Commons over recent years. But no doubt little love was lost between them. Oliver Cromwell's rich uncle (a Royalist), injured by extravagance, sold his estate to the Montagus while his nephew had moved away to Ely. When Oliver was a young man he had appeared before Henry Montagu, first Earl of Manchester, claiming that the mayor and aldermen of Huntingdon were in a position to filch the rights of the burgesses. Later, after he had been elected a member of parliament for the city of Cambridge, he supported complaints made by Manchester's tenants against their landlord over enclosures. Cromwell was said to have been passionately angry when attending a parliamentary committee on the matter and to have accused the Chairman of partiality. Cromwell always had a hot temper, which sometimes led him into trouble. By 1644, however, he had proved himself not only a born cavalry officer but also a splendid military organizer. Again and again he asserted that 'men of a spirit' could be trained to fight as well as the Royalists and he proved his point. Insisting that a man's religion had nothing to do with his military capacity, he had criticized his colleague, Major-General Crawford, who commanded the infantry for Manchester, of victimizing soldiers who were not, as he was, Presbyterian. Indeed Manchester had to take both his two subordinate commanders up to the Committee of Both Kingdoms in London before a reconciliation could be effected.

Cromwell, who was a vehement Puritan and resented Charles I's favouritism towards High Church bishops and clergy, was determined that the war should be won not merely to enforce constitutional reform but also to ensure the thorough refashioning of the English Church. Manchester, on the other hand, although he had been the principal critic of the King in the House of Lords before the war, had come to believe that the war must end not with victory but with reconciliation. He owed his position to his status and his wealth, but he was not a good general. He had disobeyed orders to send a contingent to Chester in August 1644, offering elaborate excuses for not doing so. Earlier he had rejected Cromwell's suggestion that he should organize an offensive against Newark. He was blamed for failing to launch the assault on Shaw House during the second battle of Newbury earlier than he did and for refusing to pursue the King after the battle was over. In the middle of November 1644 the Committee of Both Kingdoms significantly ordered him to keep his forces together and do nothing without the approval of a council of war of which Cromwell was a member. Later in the month Cromwell, in his capacity as a member of the Committee of Both Kingdoms and a member of parliament, asserted that Manchester had been responsible for losing the battle of Newbury on the ground that he did not want to prosecute the war 'unto a full victory' because he thought that an accommodation could be reached with the King. Furthermore Cromwell blamed Manchester for preferring to retire to Newbury rather than trying to fight the King again in order to prevent the loss of Donnington Castle; and he related that when Manchester had been urged to do so on the ground that a victory at that time would have been decisive, he retorted that 'if we beat the King ninety-nine times yet he is King still, and his posterity, and we subjects still; but if the King beat us once we should be hanged and our posterity undone'. Friends of the Earl charged Cromwell with being cruel and covetous and with favouring 'common men of poor parentage' in preference to 'honest gentlemen' for recruitment

Donnington Castle, of which the gatehouse survives, had already endured a long siege in the King's cause before October 1644. During the second battle of Newbury its guns prevented the Parliamentarian success against Prince Maurice's troops from turning into victory, and Charles was able to withdraw with his army relatively intact

to his regiment – such men were said to be 'Independents' with preaching officers and 'godly precious men' who would be sure to make a nuisance of themselves when the war ended – but Sir William Waller gave his valuable backing to Cromwell's criticisms of Manchester.

The majority in the House of Commons was impressed. Gradually it dawned on them that the failures of 1644 were principally owing to the incapacity of Essex and Manchester. It was unfortunate that they both happened to be members of the attenuated House of Lords, but it could not be helped. After Cromwell had poured out his grievances he became more tactful. Observing that the blame could not be laid upon any particular commander – indeed he had made mistakes himself – he suggested that all members of parliament who held military posts should forthwith make a self-denying gesture by resigning. Thus all suspicions of corrupt practices would be contradicted; they could start again with a clean sheet. A new army could be recruited with a new and blameless commander-in-chief. That was the right way, he believed, to win the war. Cromwell also proposed later that the Scottish army, having taken Newcastle, should be invited to come south. Naturally the House of Lords did not care for the implied aspersions on the two Earls; however the draft of the 'Self-Denying Ordinance' was amended, merely calling upon all members of parliament to resign their commands within forty days of its passing; nothing was said about their not being eligible for reappointment. After arguments stretching over four months the House of Lords was at last persuaded to agree both to the formation of what was to be known as the 'New Model Army' and to the Self-Denying Ordinance. To the general relief, before the second Ordinance was passed Essex and Manchester voluntarily laid down their commissions. Sir Thomas Fairfax, who was not a member of parliament, was on Cromwell's proposal appointed the new Lord General. He was a modest man, devoid of intrigue and a proven soldier. Harsh terms were presented to the King at a conference between representatives of the two sides held at Uxbridge in Middlesex during the first fortnight of May 1645. They required Charles to accept Presbyterianism as the national religion of England, to allow the army and navy to be permanently controlled by Parliament and also to permit Parliament to be entirely responsible for waging war against the Irish rebels. These demands were rejected with contempt. So when the campaigning season opened that spring the war was vigorously resumed.

Sir Thomas Fairfax, who was to be the young General of the New

Model Army (he was thirty-three) arrived in London from Yorkshire
in the middle of February, but it was not until April that his
appointment was approved by Parliament; thereupon he departed for
Windsor to see to the organization of this new force. The establishment for the New Model Army was 22,000 men, comprising
eleven regiments of cavalry, twelve regiments of infantry and one
regiment of dragoons, together with an artillery train. The nucleus of
the cavalry was provided from what had been the Earl of Manchester's
army, which had been largely trained by Cromwell. That was (apart
from his political activities) Cromwell's only contribution to the
creation of this army, which was Fairfax's responsibility. Over 8,000
men had to be pressed to join the infantry, which had not been
brought up to strength when the campaign began. The infantry –
musketeers and pikemen – wore red uniforms; the cavalrymen, who
were paid three times as much as the infantry (two shillings a day as
compared with eightpence) but were expected to provide their own
horses, wore light headpieces or 'pots', armour over their back and
breast and usually a buff coat of leather; their weapons were firelock
pistols and swords. Because of the mixed character of the infantry the
Royalists mocked at the New Model and anticipated no difficulty in
crushing it.

The beginnings of the campaign of 1645 are confusing because the
authorities on both sides kept on changing their minds. The King
still had hopes of making the west of England into a Royalist bastion,
whatever happened elsewhere. On 5 March he sent his eldest son, the
future Charles II, who was not yet fifteen, to be his Captain-General
in the west (with of course military and civilian advisers). The boy
Prince set up his headquarters at Bristol where he soon got into all
sorts of difficulties. To clear the ground in the west the independent-
minded Lord Goring laid siege to Taunton on 11 March for a second
time. Fairfax was duly ordered to march to the relief of Taunton at
the head of his new army while Cromwell was left to harass Oxford.
But it hardly needed a whole army to relieve Taunton any more than
when the Earl of Essex took his army to relieve Lyme the year before.
In fact Goring abandoned the siege before Fairfax could arrive, while
by the time Fairfax reached Blandford in Dorset he was recalled to
deal with a threat to the Midlands. Fairfax began his march with the
New Model Army, consisting of 10,000 infantry and 6,600 cavalry,

on 1 May. Meanwhile Prince Rupert joined the King in Oxford, thus constituting a Royalist army of nearly 12,000 men. Perturbed about where Charles might strike with this force, the Committee of Both Kingdoms then ordered Fairfax to send a detachment to relieve Taunton while he himself returned to lay siege to Oxford after the King had left there, in the expectation that this would prevent the Royalists from moving north or east – for it was not clear to the Committee which route they would choose to take.

In fact King Charles had not yet made up his mind what to do, but on 8 May he held a council of war at Stow-on-the-Wold in Gloucestershire where the decision was reached to divide his army into two parts. Lord Goring, who had been recalled from the south-west, was allowed to go back to besiege Taunton again with 3,000 cavalrymen while Rupert with the rest of the army turned north. The original idea was to fight the Scots who, because of the victory by the Marquis of Montrose at Inverlochy and his later defeat of a Covenanter force at Auldearn, a village near Nairne in northern Scotland, in the first week of May, had been obliged to reduce the size of their army in England by sending reinforcements home; after that the King might join up with Montrose. But there were alternatives. Charles and Rupert could march into East Anglia, which had been militarily weakened, or they could aim to fight the New Model before it had been thoroughly trained and blooded. It was because the Committee of Both Kingdoms was conscious of all these possibilities that it had ordered Fairfax back from the south-west to besiege Oxford and told Cromwell to leave the Oxford area and return to his home at Ely. Oliver went back expecting to be finally relieved of his commission and be able to settle down to a private life.

As instructed on 14 May, Fairfax began to besiege Oxford after having detached a brigade consisting of some 4,000–5,000 infantry and 1,800 cavalry to Taunton. Rupert now sent a message to Goring to bring back his cavalry in order to protect Oxford, but Goring thought he would soon capture Taunton and so was in no hurry to obey. So Rupert then decided that the best way to relieve the pressure on Oxford was to 'fall upon some place possessed by Parliament': Leicester, held by a weak garrison, was chosen for the purpose: on 30 May it was stormed and the next day it surrendered. The assault

'The disposition of a single regiment of infantry in the fields (according to the present discipline of His Majesty King Charles).' The colonel's quarters are in the centre (A–F), near the waggons (Q), and surrounded by the tents and huts of other officers and men; at the bottom are the huts of the sutlers, or suppliers

was brutal. Some of the defenders were slain in the heat of victory; women and children were found among the dead; the town was given over to plunder. A week later the Royalist army encamped at Daventry, twenty-five miles south of Leicester, where it collected supplies and awaited the arrival of Goring and his cavalry before advancing north again. Although Rupert affected to despise the New Model Army, he thought that discretion was the better part of valour and did not thirst for a battle.

Two days after the fall of Leicester the Committee of Both

Kingdoms, at last showing a glimpse of realism, gave Fairfax a free hand to take the offensive against the King's army. His council of war at once resolved to seek a battle. Before doing so Fairfax asked Parliament to let him appoint Oliver Cromwell as his Lieutenant-General of Horse, although his commission had expired. The Commons consented to his formal reappointment. On 13 June Oliver, with 600 cavalrymen, joined Fairfax at Kislingbury, a village eight miles east of Daventry. By then the King's army had left Daventry, where Charles had been relaxing and enjoying a spot of hunting.

The New Model Army was within six miles of the Royalists before full intelligence of its movements reached King Charles. By then his army had arrived at Market Harborough, about eighteen miles to the north-east of Daventry, and encamped there. Charles and Rupert would have liked to get farther away from the New Model Army especially as Goring had written to say that it was impossible to reinforce them immediately. But Fairfax was advancing on them too fast. That night they learned he was very near to them. Colonel Henry Ireton, Oliver Cromwell's future son-in-law, who was in charge of the Parliamentarian advance guard, actually caught a group of soldiers belonging to the Royalist rearguard as they were playing quoits or darts and drinking in the village inn at Naseby, seven miles south of Market Harborough. At midnight a council of war was called by Charles to meet in Market Harborough. Rupert was against tackling the enemy there and then, but was overruled by the King on the advice of two of his courtiers, who argued that it was dishonour-able to retreat before the New Model Army, the capacity and morale of which they underestimated. The Royalist soldiers were woken at two in the morning of 14 June to be prepared to fight, but they had to be assembled from their quarters scattered around Market Harborough and led to what we believe to be the battleground.

The village of Naseby lies almost in the centre of England. It is situated on a plateau about 200 feet above sea level; thence streams flow both to the Atlantic and to the North Sea. The plateau contains low hills and valleys; one of those who fought at the battle there wrote of 'a place of little hills and vales, the ground some ploughed, some champion [unenclosed]'. The Royalists were deployed on what was called Dust Hill, a mile south of Market Harborough, the

Parliamentarians between Fenny Hill and Mill Hill, which lie north of Naseby village, and along a line stretching 300 yards farther east. The width of each army was about a mile. The area between them, known as Broadmoor, was where the contest began.

When Prince Rupert rode out to discover the Parliamentarian dispositions he detected his enemy drawing backwards over the ridge of a hill lying to the north-west of Naseby village. He assumed they were retreating. But that was not in fact the case. The withdrawal was deliberate. Oliver Cromwell, who was with General Fairfax at the time, had advised his commander-in-chief to move back to the rear of the ridge on the ground that this would tempt the Royalists to charge uphill at them. Fairfax therefore drew up his line behind the crest of the hill.

The final layout of the two sides was therefore this: Henry Ireton, who on Cromwell's advice had been promoted to be Commissary-General, was put in command of the Parliamentarian cavalry on the left covering the north of Naseby village; the Parliamentarian infantry under Major-General Skippon were deployed in the centre; and Oliver Cromwell was in charge of the cavalry on the right, slightly ahead of the line of infantry. Cromwell also posted a dragoon regiment under Colonel Okey behind a row of hedges on the extreme left of the Parliamentarian position. Prince Rupert, although he was Captain-General of the Royalist army, personally took command of the cavalry on the right wing where his brother Prince Maurice was also stationed; the veteran Lord Astley was in charge of the infantry in the centre, which had the support of a force of cavalry; and Sir Marmaduke Langdale had a brigade of northern cavalry on the left wing of the Royalist line.

Although they took the offensive the Royalists were markedly inferior in numbers: some historians consider that they had 7,500 men, some 9,000 and some 11,000 against the 13,000 or 14,000 under Fairfax. What is certain is that Rupert had fewer cavalry; he had vainly hoped that Goring's seasoned troopers would have arrived in time to take part in the battle. Furthermore the cavalry, who came from Yorkshire under Langdale, had been mutinous, being tired of the war and anxious to go home. The Parliamentarian morale, on the other hand, was excellent. Much of the cavalry had fought for two years under Cromwell and were religiously inspired. Even the infantry had received some training when they marched into Dorset and back. In spite of low numbers and indifferent morale, Rupert opened the battle with a wide sweep to his right. Although the dragoons under Okey fired their muskets and wounded some of his men the Prince succeeded in charging uphill, defeating the Round-head regiment on the extreme left of the Parliamentarian line, and then thrust on until he reached the baggage train which covered a large area to the west of Naseby village.

Meanwhile General Ireton had halted the advance of Prince Maurice's cavalry regiment. Satisfied with this, Ireton turned to attack the right-hand side of the Royalist infantry in the centre, perceiving it was under pressure, but was wounded and temporarily taken prisoner himself.

On the left of the Royalist line the Yorkshire cavalry and Cromwell's three lines of troopers charged each other across a rabbit warren; the Royalists, being outnumbered and outflanked, were completely routed. Now, as at Marston Moor, Oliver turned his attention to the Royalist foot. Under Lord Astley, their experienced infantry commander, the Cavaliers had been thrusting forward at push of pikemen flanked by musketeers. Major-General Skippon was severely wounded, the colonel of his regiment was killed, and the whole line retreated south. Led by Fairfax himself, who then came to the rescue, the Roundhead infantry counter-attacked, but the main threat to the Royalist infantry was owing to the fact that both their wings were confronted by enemy cavalry charges: 'our foot,' a Royalist wrote afterwards, 'were left naked.' On the right they were assaulted by the remnants of Ireton's regiments and by the dragoons under Colonel Okey and on the left they were faced by such of Cromwell's cavalrymen who were not pursuing the defeated North-erners.

It was at this point in the battle that King Charles attempted to throw in his reserve, consisting of 1,500 horse and 800 foot. But in a state of utter confusion this force marched to the right instead of to the left as it should have done. By the time it was called back and was joined by Prince Rupert with his cavalry, which had returned to the battlefield from the west of Naseby, it was too late for them to save the day. As Sir Edward Walker, formerly the King's secretary-at-war, was to write in his *Brief Memorial* about the campaign of 1645, 'they

Facsimile of an engraving, by Streeter, of the battle of Naseby, 14 June 1645, seen from the Parliamentarian side. To the left of the village is the defended baggage train; above it, the left wing led by Ireton confronts cavalry led by Prince Rupert;

in the centre, the King is shown riding alone; on the right, Cromwell faces Sir
Marmaduke Langdale. The medallion in the upper right-hand corner shows Sir
Thomas Fairfax, the Parliamentarian commander-in-chief

having done their part, and not being in order . . . could never be brought to charge again, nor to rally any of the beaten troops'. This was the extraordinary end to the contest after three hours of fighting. Together Charles and his nephew retired to Leicester fourteen miles away. Part of their cavalry escaped with them, but their infantrymen, who had fought so courageously, now surrendered in droves. Some 5,000 officers and men were taken prisoner, though only a few hundred were killed in the battle. All the royal artillery and arms sufficient for 8,000 men were captured. Though the war was to continue for more than another year the Royalists' cause was ruined and their confidence undermined.

Napoleon was later to stress the value of morale in war. Even more damaging than Charles's defeat at Naseby was the capture of his cabinet containing correspondence with his wife. This disclosed the attempts that he had been making to bring over an Irish army to England and his promise of favours to Roman Catholics. The publication of these letters or drafts of letters showed the peace party on the Parliamentarian side how difficult it would be to reach any agreement with the King, and it equally strengthened the hands of the war party which wished to end the fighting with the complete and utter defeat of the Royalists.

But Charles himself, ever volatile, was not unduly depressed by the battle of Naseby. He was cheered by the continuing successes in Scotland of Montrose who, after his victory at Auldearn, marched south and again outmanoeuvred the Covenanters in a battle at Alford, twenty-five miles west of Aberdeen. The King wrote to Ormonde pressing him to send over troops from Ireland; he thought that he could recruit his infantry in Wales to replace the losses at Naseby; and he even had hopes of French assistance, for the Queen was busily intriguing on his behalf. In the west of England Lord Goring had a small but intact army engaged still on the siege of Taunton. Charles once more hesitated between trying to join Goring in Somerset or Montrose in Scotland. Neither scheme was practical. The Scots had captured Carlisle and in due course the Royalists lost both Pontefract and Scarborough, their two remaining strongholds in Yorkshire. The Scots army began moving south with the aim of besieging Hereford, Charles's temporary headquarters on the borders of Wales. Meanwhile Fairfax and Cromwell, with the victorious New

Charles, Prince of Wales, later Charles II (1630–85), became his father's Captain-General in the West in 1645. This portrait, in which he holds a commander's baton, was painted by Dobson probably to commemorate the Prince's first experience of military life at the age of twelve. With his brother James he had watched the battle of Edgehill, which is represented in the background. The left foreground is a symbolic image of the horror of rebellion

Model Army, were on their way to the relief of Taunton. The military situation was grasped by Prince Rupert who recommended the move west as the King's wisest plan, but was not sanguine about its prospects. In fact Charles went into Wales to recruit his forces and while he was doing so Goring was defeated by Fairfax.

The New Model Army, led by Fairfax, had marched rapidly from Leicester, which surrendered to him after Naseby, and by the beginning of July had reached Dorset where he pacified the Clubmen – so called because they were armed with clubs – who wanted to keep both the contending armies out of their part of the world so as to resume their peaceful occupations. As soon as Goring heard of the approach of Fairfax he gave up the siege of Taunton, ultimately drawing up his forces in a strong position covered by the rivers Yeo and Parrett which join just south of Langport in Somerset. By feinting at Taunton Goring induced Fairfax to dispatch 4,000 men there, but even then Fairfax's army outnumbered that of the Royalists. Previously by feinting at Yeovil Fairfax had managed to persuade Goring to withdraw from his forward positions. Furthermore Goring had sent off most of his artillery to Bridgwater farther west before he concentrated at Langport. So strategically all was about square between the two generals.

The battle of Langport on 10 July 1645 was a conclusive demonstration of the superior morale of the Parliamentarians. The key to the battle was a ford across a stream known as the Wagg Rhyne, a tributary of the Yeo. It was covered on the Royalist side by a ridge which could be reached solely through a narrow lane with hedges lining it. Goring posted his only two guns on top of the ridge, manned the lane with musketeers, and placed his cavalry to the rear. The Parliamentarian gunners knocked out Goring's cannon; three troops of cavalry were sent as 'a forlorn hope' to cross the ford and ride up the lane. This they managed splendidly; though checked by the Royalist cavalry, they were soon reinforced by a squadron under Major John Desborough, Oliver Cromwell's brother-in-law. After a fierce contest the Royalists broke and fled.

Surveying the situation after the battle of Langport, Prince Rupert advised the King to conclude peace. Charles replied:

If I had any other quarrel but the defence of my religion, crown and

A contemporary map of Oxford, including wider orientation, a view of the city from the east with the main landmarks indicated, and place names within the town. The badges of the university colleges are shown on either side

friends, you had full reason for your advice; for I confess that, speaking as a mere soldier or statesman, I must say there is no probability but my ruin; yet, as a Christian, I must tell you that God will not suffer rebels and traitors to prosper, nor this cause to be overthrown . . .

That was Charles at his noblest, while the letter helps to show how completely both sides believed that the Lord of Hosts would fight for them. After the defeat at Naseby the King made his way to Hereford where Prince Rupert departed from him to go to join the garrison in

Bristol. Charles himself stayed for three weeks at the fortified castle of Raglan (20 miles south of Hereford), in south Wales, which belonged to the fabulously wealthy Marquis of Worcester, to recover his spirits, and there he became optimistic, hoping to raise a new army from Wales and Ireland. Taking advantage of Cromwell's absence in the west, he daringly raided Huntingdon, Oliver's birthplace, which was given over to plunder. While he was there he learned that the heroic Montrose had crossed the Firth of Forth near Stirling to inflict another defeat on the Covenanters at Kilsyth, only ten miles north-west of Glasgow. Argyll, who was with the Covenanters, fled for safety to Berwick on Tweed, while other fugitives fled as far as Carlisle. Montrose appeared to be the master of Scotland. The Scottish army in England had no alternative but to abandon the siege of Hereford and dispatch the bulk of its cavalry home. King Charles, who had returned to Oxford after the raid on Huntingdon, was able to sally forth to Hereford to gather a new army. But soon his hopes of recovery were undermined. On 11 September Prince Rupert surrendered Bristol, the most valuable town still in the possession of the Royalists, to General Fairfax. Rupert did not have a big enough garrison to protect the five-mile circumvallation of the city, while the morale of both soldiers and civilians was at its lowest ebb. The King at once dismissed Rupert from all his offices, condemning him for a 'mean action' which tried both his faith and trust in his nephew's loyalty to his cause. But Rupert was merely accepting the military facts. Two days later Montrose was at last defeated by the reinforced Covenanters at the battle of Philiphaugh near Selkirk in the Lowlands. Those of his followers who were not killed in the battle were executed as traitors on the orders of Argyll and the Presbyterian ministers of God in the Scottish council of war. Montrose himself managed to escape to the Highlands. After Langport and Philiphaugh the first civil war was virtually over.

The King hardly knew where to turn. After enjoying the comforts of Raglan castle for another week in mid-September he marched to Chester which, though besieged by the Parliamentarians, was still held by the Royalists and was to remain in their hands until February 1646. But a force of cavalry which left the town was routed at the battle of Rowton Heath nearby on 24 September 1645. Charles then moved to Newark, also still in Royalist hands. Here undignified

Drawing of Inigo Jones (1573–1652) by Van Dyck

squabbling between Charles's advisers and courtiers broke out. Rupert arrived there on 16 October determined that the be-smirchment of his name should be removed. Under pressure Charles concurred with the findings of a council of war that his nephew had been guilty of neither cowardice nor disloyalty, but he refused to employ the Prince any more in his service.

Finally the King returned to Oxford on 5 November, having ridden 1,200 miles since he left Naseby in lengthy, tiring and largely pointless marches. Here he was to learn of the comprehensive mopping-up operations of the New Model Army in Wiltshire, Cornwall, Devon, Dorset and Hampshire. Cromwell laid siege to Basing House in Hampshire, long known as 'Loyalty House'. It was symbolic of the changed fortunes of the war that two distinguished artists formerly in the employment of the King, Wenceslaus Hollar, the engraver, and Inigo Jones, the architect, were both found there by the Parliamentarians having been engaged in planning its defences. Jones, whose responsibility for arranging the Queen's lovely masques in Whitehall Palace was not appreciated by the Puritans, was stripped naked and carried away in a blanket. Two other enduring strongholds of royalism, Hereford and Chester, also surrendered that autumn; the loss of Chester meant that all hope of succour from Ireland had to be given up by the King. Henceforward he devoted himself to elaborate diplomatic manoeuvres.

In spite of all his ingenuities the King knew in his heart of hearts that his cause was in peril. Twice he ordered his eldest son to leave England for France. Reluctantly the young Prince obeyed, eventually reaching his mother in Paris by way of the Scilly Isles and Channel Islands. His former military adviser, Lord Hopton, lingered in Cornwall for some days only to watch his remaining soldiers deserting to the other side so that he himself had to surrender honourably to Fairfax.

After the new campaigning season began in the spring of 1646 Charles escaped from Oxford in disguise and slowly found his way to the headquarters of the Scottish army, which was encamped at Southwell between Nottingham and Newark. The day after he arrived Newark surrendered to the Scots, while five days later Fairfax summoned Oxford. Articles of capitulation were finally signed on 24 June. The King's second son, the Duke of York (the future James II) thus became a prisoner of Parliament, which already held two of his sisters. The King himself was taken by the Scots to Newcastle upon Tyne where he refused either to promise the Scots to accept Presbyterianism as the dominant religion in England or to agree to

Basing House, the mansion of the Roman Catholic Marquis of Winchester, commanded the road to the west through Salisbury and had been repeatedly besieged by Parliamentarians before Cromwell overwhelmed it in October 1645. During the sacking by Cromwell's troops the house caught fire, and its fortifications were later razed

nineteen humiliating propositions sent to him from London. Instead he played golf and chess, engaged in theological arguments and procrastinated. Eventually the victorious English Parliamentarians decided to pay off the Scottish army, furnishing the first instalment of the money in January 1647. The King himself was handed over to English Commissioners who conducted him to honourable captivity at Holmby House in Northamptonshire.

Can it be said that the first civil war had any important social or economic consequences? London certainly had become more puritanical. With the departure of the Court the theatres were closed. No

The Royalist town of Newark, in Nottinghamshire, long defied the attack of
Parliamentarian armies. Prince Rupert came to its rescue in March 1644, defeating the
besiegers and capturing a vast store of artillery and supplies

longer were there masques and dancing. The King's splendid
collection of paintings was to be sold and dispersed. Long sermons
were addressed to Parliament in all times of victory or crisis.
Fast-days were frequent. London became a dismal town, especially
during the early war years suffering shortages of food and fuel, while
wounded men, war widows and orphans swelled the ranks of the city
beggars. In Oxford, on the other hand, although it was a military

Newark was once again besieged, by a combined force of English and Scottish troops, from 6 March to 8 May 1646. The defences included the town's own fortification and outworks such as the Queen's Sconce, shown here, immediately to the north-west of the town. This structure failed to help save the town and Newark was eventually surrendered, but the earthworks remain clearly visible today

headquarters, with New College turned into a magazine and cattle herded into Christ Church quadrangle, every effort was made in an overcrowded city to maintain the pomp and magnificence of the royal Court. The King appointed a Master of Revels and brought the painter William Dobson there so that he might portray members of the royal family and royal heroes such as Prince Rupert. But duels

The Royalist stronghold of Corfe Castle in Dorset was held by Lady Bankes's garrison until it fell by subterfuge in 1646. It was subsequently dismantled through the use of mining and explosives

and drunken brawls were commonplace, while the King's advisers busily intrigued against one another. Outside London and Oxford life went on much as before except in those areas where fighting was taking place. Though yeomen and smallholders are often said all to have sided with Parliament, in fact the Clubmen (who would have preferred to be neutral and vainly tried to keep the war outside the boundaries of their own particular counties) were chiefly yeomen. Some great castles such as Corfe in Dorset and Basing House in Hampshire were destroyed or left empty shells.

But the character of local government changed little. Justices of the Peace continued to function as before, while the county committees preserved law and order. Even after the Royalists had

One of the most significant events in the civil war was recorded by Ernest Crofts (1847–1911) in this work, *The surrender of the city of York to the Roundheads*, which took place after the battle of Marston Moor in 1644

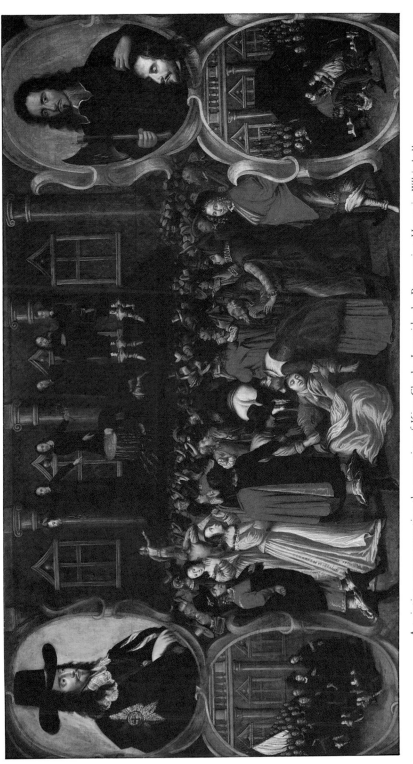

A painting commemorating the execution of King Charles I outside the Banqueting House in Whitehall palace, by an unknown artist, probably *c.* 1649. The medallion at the top left shows the monarch; that on the right, his executioner bearing the features of Lord Fairfax. Below left, the King is led to his execution, and on the right people rush to dip their handkerchiefs in the blood of the 'martyred' King been defeated there, the administration in Cornwall was carried out by exactly the same gentry class as had ruled before the war. In Suffolk, which was never Royalist, the county committee was 'a kind of exclusive club comprising much of the brains and much of the wealth of the shire'. Admittedly Royalist gentry had their lands sequestrated until fines levied upon them were paid in full. But often they quietly transferred their properties to friends who had fought on the opposite side. In the long run, modern research suggests, no significant change in the distribution of landed property took place as a result of the war.

What of the common people? They suffered most in parts of the country which were overrun by soldiers requiring food, horses and lodging paid for by 'free quarter', that is to say promissory notes. On the other hand, the demands of war created full employment and increased the earnings of labour. Some ordinary men were glad to enlist in an army or navy to secure a share of plunder. The principal grievance was the new taxes, particularly the excise which was imposed, among other things, upon ale, the chief solace of the poor. Veronica Wedgwood has observed that

> young men who had never seen anything but, at best, the parlour of some small squire's houses, now entered as conquerors some of the greatest houses in England, stared with wonder, or envy, or austere disapproval at the stately splendours of Welbeck, or Bolsover or Raglan Castle, or Lathom House . . . [yet] there is relatively little trace of vindictiveness of the poor against the rich in anything they said or did.

But freed from the authority of the Church and Royalist officials radical ideas developed and old shibboleths were questioned.

Two social consequences of the civil war may be stressed: the first is that the atmosphere of Royalist Oxford became a pattern for the dissolute and backbiting Court of Charles II where standards of sexual morality were low and of corruption high. The second is that the freedom of thought engendered both in the Parliamentarian army and among the radical sects meant that the monopolistic authority of the Church of England was permanently undermined. In the economic life of the kingdom after the Restoration the most

This triumphant piece of propaganda on the part of the Parliamentarians was produced in 1645–6 after the defeat of the Royalist armies first at Marston Moor and then at Naseby. Parliament sits in 'Englands Arke Secured' while the Royalists flounder among the 'boystrous waves': Strafford, as Lord Deputy, fires a blunderbuss in the direction of the vessel, while Newcastle valiantly waves his sword at it

significant influence was upon the growth of overseas trade. The impression of power spread abroad by the renown of the New Model Army and the Commonwealth navy paved the way for the conclusion of valuable treaties which were to pay dividends for the future British Empire.

CHAPTER SEVEN

The Second Civil War: 1648

Once the first civil war was won the effective rulers of England, who were concentrated in the House of Commons and the reduced House of Lords, had two problems before them: how to demobilize or get rid of their armies and how to come to a settlement with the defeated King. Before Charles left Newcastle he offered modified proposals, including surrendering control of the militia for ten years and accepting Presbyterianism as the national religion of England for five, though he would not take the Covenant himself. In fact he was playing for time, hoping, like Mr Micawber, that something would turn up.

In a way it did so. For after the English Parliament paid off the Scottish army and Charles was handed over to commissioners sent to fetch him from Newcastle, an opportunity for further negotiations was presented to him because differences arose between the parliamentary leaders, headed by the Presbyterian Denzil Holles, and the New Model Army. The Army was handled clumsily because it was determined that half of it should be disbanded, that the remainder should be sent to Ireland or employed on mobile policing duties in England and that apart from Fairfax no officers above the rank of colonel should be retained in service. Furthermore no member of parliament was to continue as an officer in the army and no clear provision was made about the payment of arrears or an amnesty for offences.

The New Model Army, which for the two past years had been

The Portraturs of the Comanders in Cheife of the Parlyments Forces by Sea and Land

This representation of the Parliamentarian commanders dates from the end of the first civil war. The Earl of Essex is shown as the most prominent leader, 'late General of the Parliament's Army', while Fairfax and Cromwell are shown on his left at the back of the group marching about England destroying property and living on 'free quarter', was naturally unpopular with civilians. Petitions were dispatched to Parliament asking for its prompt disbandment. But the rank-and-file of the army, owed much in the way of arrears, was unwilling to agree to demobilization or service in Ireland except on fair and acceptable conditions. Thus antagonism arose between a majority in the House of Commons and the victorious soldiers.

During the spring of 1647 three parliamentary deputations were sent to meet the army officers at Saffron Walden, then the military headquarters. The first deputation was told bluntly that more information was needed about the conditions of demobilization and the arrangements for the expedition to Ireland. That was hardly an unreasonable demand on the part of the officers; the rank-and-file at the same time drew up a petition to Fairfax seeking arrears and indemnities and asking that pensions should be paid to widows and orphans of men killed in the war. Over this petition the parliamentary majority took umbrage and in a thin House of Commons voted in favour of a declaration that those soldiers who 'in their distempered condition . . . go on advancing and promoting that petition shall be looked upon and proceeded against as enemies of the State and disturbers of the public peace'.

Such was the atmosphere of mutual distrust when the second deputation reached Saffron Walden. No concessions were offered by either side. Fairfax was instructed to order his men to volunteer for service in Ireland under Philip Skippon, a commander highly trusted in London, while the officers were told they should urge their men to volunteer. Fairfax retorted that he would express his wishes, which were usually granted, but would not issue commands; he then retired to bed with influenza at his mother-in-law's house. The officers insisted that they would do nothing until arrears had been met and an indemnity given.

At last the parliamentary leaders began to see sense. They voted that six weeks' arrears should be paid at once and they dispatched four army officers who were also members of parliament, including Cromwell, Ireton and Skippon, to treat with the army at Saffron Walden and quench its fears. They returned with the report that, provided satisfactory arrangements were made about their arrears, the soldiers would disband peaceably but would not hear of going to

Ireland. Earlier the Speaker had been told that the army was unsettled and suffering from a deep sense of its grievances; indeed the soldiers promptly observed that they were to be given only six or eight weeks' pay when more than a year's pay was owing to them. Fairfax was told that his men wanted a general meeting of the whole of the army in which each regiment should have its own representatives – known as 'adjutants' or 'agitators' – to put their point of view. Fairfax gave way and on 4 June the whole of the army camped near Newmarket. Here Cromwell as well as Fairfax joined it.

This growing hostility between Parliament and the army warmed the heart of the royal captive. Charles assured the Speaker of the House of Lords that he accepted in principle the latest proposals submitted to him, but he asked permission to come to Westminster so that he might as king give his assent to the Bills necessary to implement the agreement. Evidently he hoped now that Parliament and the army were quarrelling to be accepted as an instrument or symbol of national conciliation. But if that was his idea, it was frustrated by a *coup* organized by the army agitators. A very junior officer, Cornet Joyce, collected a force of five hundred men, marched to Holmby House, and seized the King. When Joyce was asked by Charles for his warrant, he significantly pointed to the troopers under his orders.

From the beginning of June when the King was taken into the hands of the army and when the army itself disobeyed orders to disband, the whole character of public affairs changed. Hitherto the spokesmen for the army had been content with putting forward their own specific grievances. But the attitude of Parliament chilled the soldiers' loyalty. Concessions granted to Parliament by former soldiers already disbanded (known as 'Reformadoes') and to the fathers of the City of London, who commanded a trained militia, aroused fears that a new internecine war was imminent. The New Model Army had no wish to fight Parliament but it sought a constitutional settlement which would embrace the soldiers' own claims for decent treatment now the war was over. Thus when after the seizure of the King the army leaders started drawing up declarations, a move was made towards framing political proposals. These proposals may well be linked with the evolution of the Leveller movement, led by John Lilburne, himself a former Lieutenant-

Colonel, whose 'large petition' published in March 1647 had social and economic overtones. Cromwell and other principal army officers might still aver that the settlement of the kingdom should be left to Parliament and that 'when the State has once made a settlement we [soldiers] have nothing to say but submit and suffer', but they were being gradually driven to taking up a more positive attitude: a 'Declaration of the Army' dated 15 June, drawn up by the Council of the Army, which included representatives of the rank-and-file as well as officers, claimed the army's right to speak in the name of the English people since it was not 'a mere mercenary army hired to serve any arbitrary power of a State, but called forth and conjured by several declarations of Parliament to the defence of their own and the people's just rights and liberties'. Parliament was therefore required

Parliamentarian soldiers in Yorkshire following Puritan procedure – destroying 'Popish' paintings and altar furniture, and smashing the communion rails which separated the congregation from the altar

to purge itself of obnoxious members and to fix a date for its own dissolution.

It is not possible to describe in detail the political and constitutional arguments of the different sides which were reproduced in pamphlets and broadsheets during the rest of 1647. But first should be considered the position of the King whose actions brought about the second war. While he was a prisoner of the army he went on negotiating, auctioneering, as it were, the value of his services to the community. At one time he rejected the draft proposals put forward by the army in a document drawn up largely by Henry Ireton known as *The Heads of the Proposals*. Later Charles accepted this as a basis for discussion and it was indeed modified in an attempt to satisfy him. At the same time a number of prominent Scotsmen, including the first Duke of Hamilton and the Earl of Lauderdale, were offering to help Charles back to authority provided he met their religious demands. To Cromwell and Ireton the King promised toleration of religious dissenters; to the Scots, on the contrary, he spoke of suppressing the sects. While the Council of the Army was considering fresh political schemes Charles escaped from imprisonment in Hampton Court, where he had been moved by the army, and fled to the Isle of Wight. Evidently he imagined that he would obtain a freer hand in negotiating there and that if the worst came to the worst he could find a ship and leave for France. But his attempts to escape were to prove abortive. Finally he consented to the Scots' religious requirements. He agreed to the establishment of a Presbyterian system for three years, to allow an assembly of divines to draw up a permanent settlement for the Church, and to put down the Independents and other sects. In return the Scots engaged to restore him safe and free to his throne.

Before that engagement was reached the English military commanders had decided to coerce Parliament. On 6 August the army entered London and eleven of the leaders in the Commons who had been most critical of the soldiers fled. The army then withdrew to Putney, a few miles from Westminster, to reconsider the whole political situation. Under Leveller influence a republican movement was beginning to emerge, though this was not specifically stated. Cromwell, who took the chair at army debates held in Putney, was willing to come to terms with the King if that was the only effective

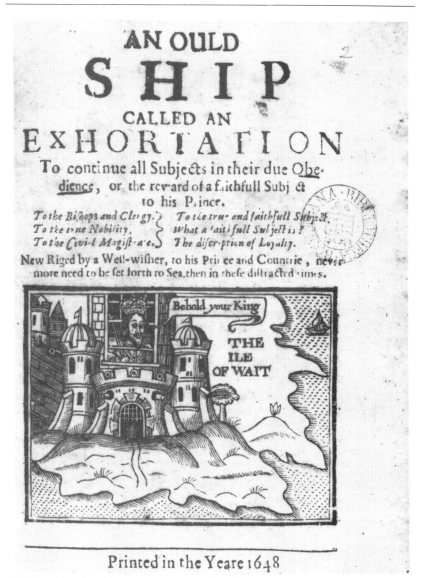

AN OULD
SHIP
CALLED AN
EXHORTATION

To continue all Subjects in their due Obedience, or the reward of a faithfull Subj &
to his Prince.

To the Bishops and Clergy. To the true and faithfull Subject.
To the true Nobility, What a faithfull Subject is?
To the Civil Magistrate. The description of Loyalty.

New Riged by a Well-wisher, to his Prince and Countrie, never
more need to be set forth to Sea, then in these distracted times.

Behold your King

THE ILE OF WAIT

Printed in the Yeare 1648

This Royalist print shows the King in Carisbrooke Castle on the Isle of Wight, where he
fled to in November 1647 in search of freedom after his escape from Hampton Court.
When he left it in December 1648 after a year's imprisonment in the castle, it was to
stand trial for his life

means of restoring peace and order to the country. On 20 October 1647 he delivered a three-hour speech in the Commons opposing a motion that no further negotiations should take place unless Charles accepted the rigorous terms put to him at Newcastle and elsewhere. However once it became known at the end of the year that Charles, after fleeing to the Isle of Wight, had come to a secret arrangement with the Scots Commissioners, who engaged themselves in return for promises he made to them to invade England on his behalf, Parliamentarians and army officers closed their ranks. A vote was carried in the Commons to stop negotiations with the King and orders were given that he should be subjected to closer surveillance.

What were the immediate causes of the second civil war? Undoubtedly the failure of the English political nation to conclude a settlement with the King was the main factor. Though the republican movement had been strengthened by the course of events and there was talk of impeaching and deposing Charles I, more people adhered to the view that the monarchy must remain the headstone of satisfactory government. Secondly, two sources of resentment prevailed. The first was growing dissatisfaction with the imposition of Puritanism in its most disagreeable and censorious forms. The second was the unpopularity of many county committees which had been set up during the first civil war to raise money and recruit soldiers, afterwards being given powers to sequester and administer Royalist estates.

As local historians have pointed out, the county committee 'had no clearly defined authority over the civil population', but 'civil and military affairs were so closely entangled that it could not avoid taking upon itself the solution of many overtly civil problems'. Moreover since usually the Clerk of the Peace and Justices of the Peace in sympathy with Parliament were members of the committee, in effect they came to rule as a kind of local oligarchy. Sometimes a virtual dictatorship emerged. In Kent Sir Anthony Welden, an elderly, bitter and disappointed man, was the local boss and so was a Puritan extremist, Sir John Pyne, in Somerset. Thus a rising which took place in Kent in the spring of 1648 was not so much positively Royalist as an active protest against 'the thing called a committee'. That was why it was supported by 'nearly all the indigenous Kentish families who had formed the backbone of the moderate party since

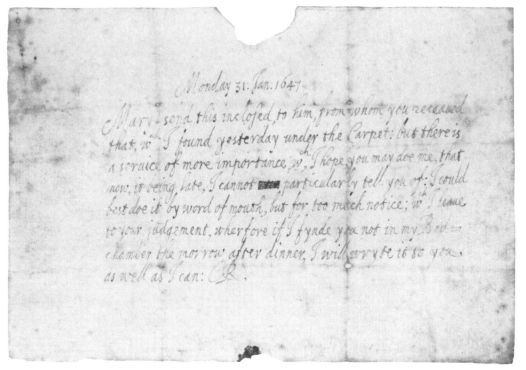

The King repeatedly planned his escape from Carisbrooke, smuggling letters out via his chambermaid Mary. The note shown here was written on 31 January 1648 (1647 by the old calendar), when the King had been a prisoner for exactly a month

1640'. But it was because the intensity of grievances against the Parliamentarian regime varied from county to county that the Royalists proved incapable of co-ordinating revolts in the second civil war. The numerous rebels in Kent failed to come to an agreement with the Royalists in neighbouring Essex; the consequence was that the Kentish rising was put down by General Fairfax almost before the men of Essex took up their arms. Similarly the discontented citizens in London were not approached by George Goring, Earl of Norwich, who had been sent to take control in south-east England, until the necessary military precautions to suppress an outbreak had been completed. Though half the navy declared itself for the King in July, Charles, Prince of Wales, who took command of the revolted

Engraved title-page of *Mercurius Rusticus*, the Royalist newspaper. The 'sad Events of the later unparraleld Rebellion' included the fortification of Oxford and Cambridge, the plundering of three great houses and the humiliation of ministers of religion (one is forced to ride on a bear)

warships, failed to succour the risings in Kent or Essex. Finally Royalist defenders of the city of Colchester, who gallantly held out against Fairfax for ten weeks, were already at their last gasp by the time the news of the defeat of the Scottish 'Engagers' in Lancashire reached them. Thus whereas the Royalists in the first civil war survived so long against the superior resources and arms of Parliament because they enjoyed central direction from the King, in the second civil war Parliamentarian armies were skilfully marshalled by Fairfax while the Royalist military effort lacked unity, for the King was a closely guarded prisoner and Prince Rupert, who had returned to Holland, was no longer able to guide strategy or to infuse his energy into the war.

The scattered risings which reflected a reaction in favour of the King had begun when on 9 April the Lord Mayor of London sent a party of militia to prevent a crowd of boys from playing tip-cat in Moorfields on the Sabbath day. A crowd of apprentices took the side of the boys and marched along Fleet Street and the Strand towards Whitehall. Cromwell ordered his cavalry to charge the mob, which was forced to break up. But the episode was a warning of the temper of ordinary people in the City. A not dissimilar riot had taken place in Canterbury at Christmas 1647 when the Mayor had forbidden the usual festivities and tried to compel the shops to stay open. His orders were defied, holly bushes placed at street doors, and cries were heard of the need to release the King. Though, as in London, the military suppressed the riot after ten days, the discontent of even moderate men presaged the rebellion in Kent in the early spring. Such were the sort of demonstrations in England. In South Wales during April the colonel in command of Pembroke Castle aroused the county and declared for the King and the Book of Common Prayer. By May it was learnt in London that the Engagers in Scotland were mobilizing an army and by the end of the month an attempt by King Charles to escape from the Isle of Wight was known to have taken place and to have failed. In the middle of the month there were stirrings in Surrey as well as Kent, but by 1 June Fairfax had occupied the county capital of Maidstone and the Kentish field force of some 8,000 volunteers, headed by men recently released from prison, was dispersed, only 500 getting away to Rochester, eventually to join the Essex Royalists under the command of the Earl of Norwich.

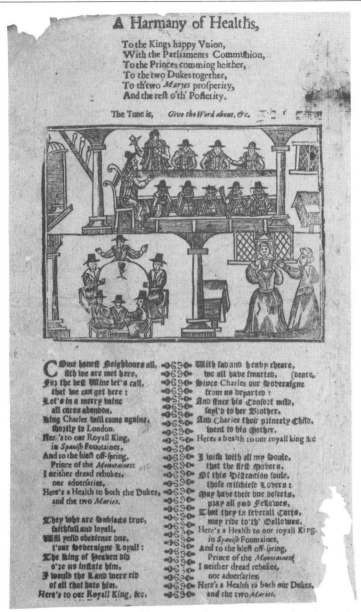

Popular sentiment was often roused by the use of printed propaganda and songsheets such as *A Harmany of Healths*. This Royalist songsheet was printed in London and expresses support for the King, for 'the blest off-spring' (the Prince of Wales) and other Royalist leaders, and wishes death on the gallows to 'the first Movers of this Distraction foule'

Charles I and James, Duke of York, during the period in which the King was imprisoned at Hampton Court, *c.* 1647, painted by Sir Peter Lely

At this very time a Royalist force in the north of England had gathered under the command of Sir Marmaduke Langdale, who after occupying Carlisle organized the capture of Pontefract Castle by a stratagem. Later Royalists occupied Scarborough Castle. Major-General John Lambert, who had been the Parliamentarian commander in the north since the previous summer, was obliged to send a detachment to besiege Pontefract Castle, while he himself watched

Langdale's movements in Cumberland. Thus for a while the Royalists held Rochester, Dover, Deal, Chelmsford, Pembroke, Pontefract, Scarborough and Carlisle while unrest showed itself in the City of London and permeated the fleet stationed in the Downs.

The most remarkable victory of the second civil war was the battle-and-rout of Preston, and the most dramatic episode was the defence of Colchester by the Royalists. Cromwell, after some difficulties owing to the temporary loss of his siege-guns in the mud of the Severn, defeated the rebel colonel and occupied Pembroke Castle on 11 July. Three days earlier the Duke of Hamilton and the Scottish Engagers had entered England and begun to march south via Carlisle and Preston, aiming for Manchester and North Wales. Fairfax ordered Cromwell to join Lambert in the north. By mid August Oliver, pausing only to reinforce the troops besieging Pontefract, marched his army at the rate of ten miles a day and linked up with Lambert at Otley near Leeds in Yorkshire. Neither side really knew what the other was doing. Hamilton finally decided not to go into Yorkshire but to continue his march through Lancashire. Besides his army of some 9,000 to 10,000 Scots, Langdale commanded 3,000 or 4,000 English Royalists while Sir George Monro managed to bring 2,100 foot and 1,200 horse across the Irish sea to fight for the King. As Hamilton was reinforced by another 4,000 raised in Scotland within a month of his own departure, the Scots and Royalists in the north amounted to over 20,000 men. The Parliamentarian army under Cromwell and Lambert consisted of only about 9,000, but they were more experienced and with a higher morale than their enemy. The Scots were inadequately armed and provisioned, they were encumbered by women camp-followers and the weather was unpleasant in the extreme. Cromwell was informed incorrectly that Hamilton was waiting at Preston for the arrival of Monro's men. On 16 August after holding a council of war in the Pennines, which divide Yorkshire from Lancashire, Cromwell resolved to advance along the north bank of the River Ribble so as to cut off Hamilton from his base in Scotland.

As it happened, by the time the Parliamentarians reached Preston Moor to the north of the town the bulk of the Scottish army had already crossed the Ribble, while Langton with his 3,000 or 4,000 men remained in Preston as a kind of flank or rearguard. Although

Sir Marmaduke Langdale (1598–1661), whose cavalry was routed by Cromwell at Naseby. He later led a successful campaign in the north, capturing Carlisle and Pontefract Castle in 1648

several reports had reached him of the proximity of the enemy he appears to have been under the impression that Cromwell had divided his force with the aim of halting Hamilton in Manchester or even that he would only have to deal with the Lancashire militia. Langdale's troops were strung across a narrow lane amidst hedges and ditches. Thus it was essentially an infantry battle which took place, and lasted for four hours. Slowly Langdale's men were pushed back and eventually the Parliamentarian horse thrust their way into the lane to occupy Preston town.

The Duke of Hamilton himself had fought bravely in the battle, but he had left it too late to recall any except a few Scottish lancers to reinforce Langdale. The Scots continued their way southwards through the mud and rain, losing stragglers on the road as Cromwell pursued them after the victory. 'The faint and weary soldiers' who 'lagged behind,' wrote a Scottish officer, 'we never saw again'. They even had to abandon much of their ammunition; they did not dare to make a stand, but after another night march on 18/19 August they aimed to reach Warrington in Lancashire where they hoped to confront their pursuers along the line of the River Mersey. But Cromwell trapped them at Winwick, three miles north of Warrington, where after a vain stand the Scots lost many killed or taken prisoner. Later that day the remains of the Scottish infantry surrendered at Warrington. The Scottish cavalry rode on towards Chester and North Wales, but finally Lambert caught up with them on 25 August at Uttoxeter in Staffordshire, where Hamilton himself surrendered. Meanwhile Cromwell had mopped up the stragglers and compelled Monro and his men from Ireland to retreat hastily into Scotland where they met a grim fate. By the first week of October Cromwell, having secured the vital towns of Carlisle and Berwick, was himself in Scotland. He had little difficulty in coming to terms with Argyll, who had been opposed to the enterprise of Hamilton and his Engagers. In Edinburgh it was readily agreed that the Engagers should be removed from all offices of trust; Cromwell left Lambert with three regiments as a kind of miniature army of occupation north of the Tweed.

The story of the siege of Colchester, as related by Matthew Carter who took part in it as the King's Quartermaster-General, reveals the loyalty that King Charles I could still inspire. The five hundred men

A detail from a plan of the siege of Colchester, which ended in the town's surrender to Fairfax on 27 August 1648. On all but the side protected by the river Parliamentarian siege-works surround the town, still largely contained within its medieval walls. Buildings outside the walls suffered heavily; disastrously for the besieged, they included the town waterworks and mills (two watermills are shown on the river, to the east)

who after many adventures had escaped from Maidstone and patiently awaited the return of their commander-in-chief, the Earl of Norwich, from the east of London, were joined at Chelmsford in Essex by a party of fifty gentlemen who had met at Hyde Park Corner and marched through the night by way of Epping having lost only one man and one horse, both of whom were later recovered. Then after collecting arms and provisions they linked up with the Royalists of Essex, whereby, wrote Carter, 'there was Unity of the Engagement, as well as of Interest, and the greater Hopes of Success'. All told, this Royalist force numbered some 4,000 men. On 13 June it was learnt

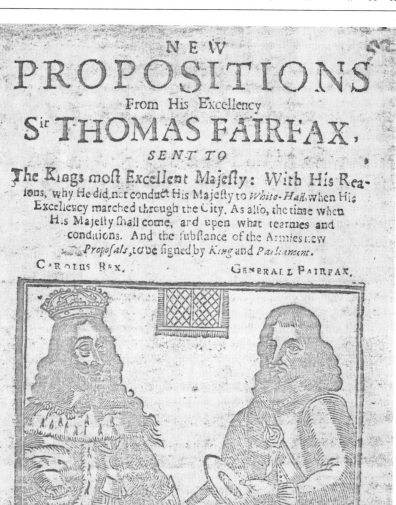

NEW
PROPOSITIONS
From His Excellency
Sᵣ THOMAS FAIRFAX,
SENT TO

The Kings most Excellent Majesty: With His Reasons, why He did not conduct His Majesty to *White-Hall,* when His Excellency marched through the City. As also, the time when His Majesty shall come, and upon what tearmes and conditions. And the substance of the Armies new *Proposals,* to be signed by *King* and *Parliament.*

CAROLUS REX.   GENERALL FAIRFAX.

Printed at *Oxford* by *Leonard Brown,* and Reprinted at *London* for *Robert Williams, Anno Dom.* 1647.

Sir Thomas Fairfax was a committed Parliamentarian, anxious for a constitutional settlement with King Charles I, as illustrated above, but was opposed to his execution that Fairfax, with 5,000 men, was hard on their heels when they made what was intended to be only a temporary halt in Colchester. The Parliamentarian army thrust its way through one of the city gates counting on a quick victory as at Maidstone, but was eventually driven out with the loss of 700 men; they left, wrote Carter, 'their Bodies in the Streets and Hedges, as infallible witnesses of what had been done; yawning out their Souls to receive their Arrears in another World, for their religious rebellion in this'. Impressed by his casualties, Thomas Fairfax decided to subject the town to a regular siege, building lines of circumvallation and aiming to starve the garrison into surrender.

An able group of Royalist officers, including Lord Norwich, Sir Charles Lucas, an Essex man, Sir George Lisle and Lord Capel, organized the defence. Though undertaking one sally to relieve the pressure, the besieged were gradually hemmed in. Most of the mills used to grind corn for bread were destroyed; on 20 July the garrison started eating their horses; later they consumed the cats and dogs in the town. To begin with, all the courtesies were observed, but propaganda was employed. As soon as the news of Cromwell's victory at Preston was known to them, the council of war in Colchester decided to surrender on stiff terms. The rank-and-file were promised 'fair quarter' but the officers had to 'surrender to mercy'. Provoked by such a long resistance, Fairfax and his council of war decided as 'some satisfaction of military justice' to shoot two Royalist officers, Sir Charles Lucas, who had been the soul of the defence, and Sir George Lisle. It is likely that Colonel Henry Ireton, who had taken part in the siege and was one of the three officers who witnessed the shooting, inspired the decision, for he was a stern man. But it was Fairfax's responsibility. Lucas and Lisle paid for their loyalty with their lives. It was not a deed done in hot blood, such as was to be performed at Drogheda in Ireland when the garrison refused to surrender after a breach had been blown in the walls, nor at that stage was it likely to offer a terrible example in order to bring about a speedy ending to the war, for the war had already been won. Twelve years later Fairfax himself was to take up arms in order to restore King Charles II to his throne.

As soon as the second civil war finished Parliament, reinforced by men like Denzil Holles, who had earlier fled to France to avoid the

Carnifex Maiestatis Regis Angliæ.

Fairfax as the King's executioner, in an engraving of *c.* 1649. In actual fact, Fairfax refused to approve the King's beheading and was to help restore his son wrath of the army, decided to repeal the vote of no addresses and to reopen negotiations with the King in the Isle of Wight. A commission, consisting chiefly of members of the old peace party and moderates, met Charles at Newport, the capital of the Isle of Wight, and entered upon leisurely discussions. But many men inside and outside the army were no longer disposed to trust the King once he had called in the Scottish Engagers. Petitions were sent to London from the counties seeking 'impartial justice' on all concerned with launching the second civil war. Charles recognized the danger of his position; he agreed at last that Parliament should control the armed forces for twenty years; but he still would not accept a permanent Presbyterian establishment for the English Church.

Meanwhile a republican movement was growing. Colonel Edmund Ludlow, who was one of its protagonists, went to see Fairfax at Colchester early in September to complain to him about the reopening of negotiations with the King. Fairfax was non-committal. Ludlow was received more sympathetically by Ireton. The proposal

A facsimile of the King's death-warrant. The signatures include Bradshaw's and Cromwell's in the first column, and Ireton's and Mauleverer's in the second

Informative, contemporary Dutch engraving of the execution of Charles I: the roles of
the main characters involved are indicated in the key, top left. The King is seen handing
his George – the insignia of the Order of the Garter – to Juxon, the Bishop of London,
before kneeling at the block

that came to be adumbrated was to purge Parliament of the peace
party or even forcibly to dissolve it. Ireton, dissatisfied with Fairfax,
thought of resigning from the army and at the end of the month he
resumed his seat in the Commons. But he soon realized that if he
wanted to stop the negotiations with the King, he must exert his
influence with Fairfax and the army rather than deliver speeches at
Westminster. Therefore he drew up a long 'remonstrance' which he
wanted the army to submit to Parliament asking for constitutional
reforms and demanding that in order to ensure the safety of the
people as a whole the King should be brought to trial. At the same
time Ireton's and other regiments were seeking 'impartial justice' and
the immediate dissolution of Parliament. Ireton tried to make the
remonstrance palatable to the Levellers, although they afterwards

claimed that they did not want the King to be put on trial before a new constitution had been agreed upon. However the council of officers meeting at St Albans on 18 November accepted the remonstrance in principle. Captain (formerly Cornet) Joyce went up to Yorkshire to see Cromwell and bring him the news of the grave decision taken at St Albans.

Both Cromwell and Fairfax were carried along by the tide. Fairfax was reluctantly convinced that the King must be deposed and he led his army into London to coerce Parliament for a second time. Cromwell would have preferred to induce the House of Commons to change its mind about negotiating further with the King rather than expel the members of the peace party there. But Ireton and Ludlow, together with Colonel Pride, a former brewer, thought differently. When the Commons had refused to hear the army's remonstrance and voted in effect to go on treating with the King, these officers carried out a 'purge'. Forty-five members of parliament were put under arrest and 120 others, who had voted in favour of continuing the Newport negotiations, were secluded from the House while 160 more voluntarily withdrew. It was this drastically purged House of Commons which voted in December that the negotiations of Newport were 'highly dishonourable and destructive of the peace of the kingdom' and ten days later appointed a committee to consider how to 'proceed by way of justice' against the King. On 1 January 1649 an ordinance was passed by the Commons instituting a high court specifically to try the King. On 27 January 1649 Charles was condemned to death by sixty-nine members of the court as a tyrant and a traitor who had shed the blood of his own people. In addressing the monarch, who was sentenced to death, the President of the court, John Bradshaw, asserted that the King was subject to the law and that the law proceeded from Parliament. But Charles remained adamant to the end. Speaking to the group round the scaffold in Whitehall three days later, he said:

Truly I desire their [the people's] liberty and freedom as much as anybody whomsoever; but I must tell you their liberty and freedom consists in having of government those laws by which their life and their goods may be most their own. It is not for having a share in government . . .

Though he was then beheaded, the Stuart dynasty was not destroyed. During the first week of February the Prince of Wales, now nineteen years old, who was safely in Holland, was told the news of his father's execution and assumed the title of King Charles II. Owing to the unscrupulous methods he used to regain his throne a third civil war came about.

CHAPTER EIGHT

The Third Civil
War: 1649–1651

Charles II and his exiled Court had now to decide how to overthrow
the 'Free Commonwealth', or rather republic, which was in the
process of being established in England after the execution of the
martyred monarch, and thus to regain the throne of the Stuarts in the
Palace of Whitehall. Three possible courses presented themselves.
The first was to rely on foreign help. Charles II was an honoured
guest in Holland where his brother-in-law, William II, was Stadthol-
der and Captain-General. So long as he could maintain his authority
and influence the Dutch Prince would give every assistance he could
to the exiled King. But William quarrelled with the Regents of
Amsterdam and soon afterwards died of smallpox, leaving a post-
humous child as his heir. Thus the United Netherlands came to be
ruled by an oligarchy, just as England was, for the remnants of the
victorious House of Commons had assumed full sovereign rights.
Other monarchs expressed their sympathies for Charles II, doling out
small sums of money as tokens of concern. But though Charles's
mother was the aunt of Louis XIV, the French Regency had its hands
full with a civil war of its own as well as a war with Spain, while the
Spaniards, fearful of English naval might, were the first to recognize
the Commonwealth Government. So in fact no immediate aid of any
significance was available to the Royalists from European powers.

The second possibility open to Charles II was an invasion of
England from Ireland and the third was an invasion from Scotland.
The Royalists still living in England were crushed, mulcted with

Pro-Commonwealth propaganda, with the caption 'No King   No Popery   Liberty
Cromwell for ever'

heavy fines and depressed after the second civil war, their activities
being closely watched by the county committees. However it was
reasonable to suppose that if an invading army arrived by sea or by
land they would again rally to the cause. The difficulty here was that
both the Irish and the Scots were divided among themselves. It is
true that a fortnight before the execution of Charles I the devoted
Marquis of Ormonde, the King's Lord-Lieutenant, had succeeded in
concluding a treaty at Kilkenny between the Royalists and the
Supreme Council of the Confederate Irish by which in return for the
grant of the free exercise of Roman Catholicism and the independence

Another of Grebner's predictions: the mole in the coffin is purported to be Cromwell, surrounded by his Parliamentarian supporters; the victorious lion is Charles, about whom we are told by Lilly: 'The Late King *Charles* was he signified by the *Lion*. After him is imported there shall no more Kings succeed in *England*. He had the signe *leo* ascending in his Nativity, one maine cause, which made him so obstinate.'

King Charles II was crowned at the traditional Scottish coronation place of Scone on
1 January 1651

of the Irish Parliament the confederates promised to supply Ormonde
with an army of over 15,000 men. Thus the Lord-Lieutenant might
hope to wipe out such few soldiers loyal to the English Parliament as
there were in Ireland and to convert the island into a base from which
England could be invaded. That this was a practical policy was
indicated by the ease with which, six months earlier, Colonel George
Monro had been able to land troops from Ulster in western Scotland
to join in the disastrous Preston campaign. The Scots for their part

Another example of Royalist propaganda against the republican Commonwealth,
represented by the figure of a griffon – contrasting with the monarchy and Church which
enshrine the liberties gained by Magna Carta

were divided between the Covenanters who looked to the astute and
pious Argyll for leadership, the surviving Engagers whose heads, the
second Duke of Hamilton and the Earl of Lauderdale, had been
banished after the campaign of 1648 and were now with Charles II in
exile, and the Royalists, mainly concentrated in the Highlands,
whose hero was the Marquis of Montrose.

The Covenanters, angry with an English Parliament for having
had the impertinence to execute a Scottish monarch, proclaimed
Charles II as King on 5 February 1649. On 22 February Charles
appointed Montrose as his Captain-General in Scotland with instructions to form the nucleus of an army with which to recruit the
Highland clans. But Charles's immediate hopes were fixed on
Ireland; even before his father's death Ormonde had invited him to
come there so that he might direct an invasion of England. But it was
not until the middle of September that Charles reached Jersey in

preparation for going on to Ireland. Ormonde had again urged him
to come, since he was aware that the confederate Irish were more
concerned with securing their own liberties than with actually
assisting the King. Ormonde thought that only the presence of
Charles in Dublin would unite the Irish in his cause. In fact by the
time Charles was ready to land there it was too late: knowing what
was on foot, the English Parliament persuaded Oliver Cromwell to
go to Ireland as its Lord-Lieutenant and Captain-General to punish
the native Irish for their rebellion in 1641 and to overthrow the
Royalists there. Even before Cromwell's arrival with a well-paid and
well-provisioned army Ormonde's troops had been defeated at the
battle of Rathmines near Dublin (2 August 1649), while on
3 September Cromwell crushed and largely slaughtered the garrison
of the key town of Drogheda in Leinster which consisted partly of
Royalists and partly of native Irish. While Charles was in Jersey
Cromwell subdued much of Munster, the principal home of Irish
Royalists. Ormonde wrote to the King telling him that without
considerable sums of money he could not raise another army after
these defeats nor advise Charles to continue on his way from Jersey.
The fact that substantial numbers of Englishmen fighting in Ireland
had changed sides to enlist in Cromwell's army, while the native
Irish were terrified, revealed that the hope of restoring the King to
his throne in England with the help of a combined Irish army was
negligible.

After learning the bad news from Ireland Charles left Jersey in
February 1650. The victorious Parliamentarian commander returned
to London at the end of May, leaving an army of occupation under
the command of his son-in-law, Ireton. The King now felt that he
had no alternative but to listen to the stringent terms which the Scots
required him to accept before they would allow him to come to
Scotland. When in March 1649 Commissioners had arrived in
Holland to see their new King, he had refused to commit himself to
them and played for time, hoping for a victory in Ireland and help
from Montrose. Now, a year later, Charles entered into negotiations
with fresh Scottish Commissioners who met him at Breda. The
Committee of Estates, which ruled Scotland, insisted upon stiff and
uncompromising terms; even Argyll thought that they went too far.
But Charles was pressed by his brother-in-law William II to agree to

Charles II dancing with his sister Mary at a ball at The Hague, painted by the Dutch artist Cornelius Janssen (1590–1665). In the background Queen Henrietta Maria and Queen Elizabeth of Bohemia look on; the boy with them is the future William III

them. After six weeks of arguing and diplomatic manoeuvring he signed, on 1 May 1650, a draft agreement known as the Treaty of Breda. By this Charles in effect promised to swear to the two Covenants, which committed him to impose a Presbyterian system on England as well as Scotland, to recognize the legality of the purged Scottish Parliament, to repudiate his arrangements with Ormonde and Montrose and to forbid the exercise of the Roman Catholic religion anywhere in his dominions. In return all that the Scottish Commissioners offered was formally to invite Charles to Scotland to be crowned King and to give verbal assurances that the Engagers would be restored at least to their personal rights as subjects. The Commissioners did not really trust Charles to fulfil all his promises, but they believed they had him in a cleft stick. A

THE SCOTS HOLDING THEIR YOVNG KINGES NOSE TO Ý GRINSTO
Come to the Grinstone Charles tie now to late :
To Recolect tis presbiterian fate :
You Covinant pretenders must Ibee
The subiect of Youer Tradgie Comedie :
Jockie
Stoope Charles :

A cartoon from a broadsheet of 1651 attacks both the Scots and Charles II, whom it sees as taking advantage of each other – Charles by feigning sympathy for the Presbyterian Kirk, the Scots by using Charles as an excuse to invade England

well-informed reporter at Breda thought that on one side the King would never 'prove a strenuous defender of their [the Scottish] faith', while on the other the Scots at heart hated monarchy and merely intended to use Charles as a figurehead for their own ends. Thus the Covenanters neither then nor after Charles's arrival in Scotland on 23 June committed themselves to fighting for his restoration to the English throne. Yet it was because Charles reluctantly went to Scotland that the third civil war came about.

The very day after Charles landed the Council of State in London debated the question whether in the interests of the security of the Commonwealth Scotland should be invaded by an English army. It has to be remembered that, although England and Scotland have now been politically united as one kingdom for nearly three hundred years, in the mid-seventeenth century the Scots were regarded by the English not as fellow subjects of the Stuarts but as national enemies. Only two years earlier a Scots army had invaded England in an attempt to restore a Scots king to power there. The Council of State therefore decided to launch a preventive war by ordering Lord Fairfax to lead an army into Scotland; for the majority of the members were convinced that if that were not done a Scots army, headed by Charles II, would be crossing the northern frontier. They were both right and wrong; for while Charles was in fact to move into England in the following year, in the summer of 1650 Argyll and the dominant Covenanters had no intention of doing so. Fairfax demurred. He said if the Scots attacked England he would lay down his life in opposing them, but he refused to make war on a people between whom and the English Parliament there still existed a Solemn League and Covenant; the Councillors were not unduly concerned over subtle differences between the Scottish Covenanters and the Scottish Engagers. But Fairfax was adamant in refusing the command; Cromwell, who had returned from Ireland at the end of May, was appointed in his place.

It is often assumed that Fairfax was a softer and milder character than Cromwell. But in fact his shooting of the two knights at Colchester in 1648 and the fierceness with which he suppressed army mutinies in 1649 show that he was stern and tough. He had refused to take any oath to the Commonwealth which would have meant giving his approval to the trial and execution of Charles I. Under the influence of his wife, who was both Presbyterian and Royalist, Fairfax was becoming alienated from the new regime and glad to wash his hands of it. Cromwell therefore, on 22 July, led an army of some 16,000 men over the Tweed'; by the middle of August he was attempting to surround and cut off Edinburgh. The war of manoeuvre – Cromwell was opposed by a large Covenanting army under David Leslie, who had fought with him at Marston Moor – was accompanied by a war of propaganda. Cromwell claimed that by welcoming the light-hearted Charles II into their bosoms the Scots were fighting against 'the very power of godliness and holiness'. To this the Scots retorted by obliging Charles to declare that his father had been guilty in resisting the reformation of the Church of England and that his mother was an idolatress. Thus Charles too became godly

The Royall Oake of Brittayne is an allegory of the King's execution. Cromwell, whose motives are pictured as being entirely mercenary, uses 'diabolical inspiration' to encourage the people in the destruction of their King and state institutions: the Church, the Crown and the Common Law which rest in the oak's branches

and holy. However he remarked in confidence that he remained at heart a true child of the Anglican Church and a true Cavalier. Indeed he used every resource and any lie to rekindle the civil wars.

On 3 September Cromwell won a major victory over the Scots at Dunbar. Anxious to prove that they were fighting for their religion and their country rather than in the cause of 'a malignant king', Commissioners for Purging appointed by the Committee of Estates were expelling unpurified (and experienced) soldiers from Leslie's army up to the eve of the battle. Furthermore Leslie was induced through the influence of the Kirk to move his army off the impregnable position it had taken up on Doon Hill, two miles from the port of Dunbar, which was the English base, forward on to the rich sloping grasslands below the line of the Lammermuir Hills so as to be able to fall like Ehud upon the Moabites.

Observing this, Cromwell and his fellow generals decided to attack at dawn on the following day the new strung-out Scottish position stretching from the hills down towards the sea. This involved one of the hardest manoeuvres in war, an attack beginning in the dark, preceded by the crossing of a natural obstacle, in this case a steep and slippery glen or trough which protected the Scottish right. What it did not involve, as has often been asserted, was an attack directed mainly by English infantrymen on the Scottish cavalry which formed the right flank of their long line. Cromwell knew better than any man that except in wooded country pikemen and musketeers stood little chance against mounted and armoured men. The assault was launched against the Scottish right by six cavalry regiments led by Major-General Lambert and Lieutenant-General Fleetwood, while Colonel Monck with a brigade of foot attacked the Scottish infantry in the centre. The Scots were by no means completely surprised, but after a night spent without cover in wet cornfields they were somewhat demoralized. Nevertheless, as Cromwell was to report, 'the enemy made a gallant resistance, and there was a very hot dispute at sword's point between our horse and theirs'. Cromwell then sent in his reserves – his own regiment of horse and three regiments of foot. The foot regiments repulsed the finest of the Scottish infantry at push of pike, while the cavalry helped to rout Leslie's right wing. After stiff resistance on their right and centre the Scots panicked and threw down their arms and their left wing, hemmed in at the base of the hills where it had been contained by a mere demonstration, disintegrated. The English took 10,000 prisoners, about half of the Scottish army, and killed 3,000, while their own losses were small. This battle was not strictly part of the third civil war, for it was a national conflict, but because of it the young King was able, after he had been crowned at Scone on 1 January 1651, to revive Scottish Royalism and meld it with that of English sympathizers in the north to engage on one last great battle between Cavaliers and Roundheads.

The battle of Dunbar, 3 September 1650. Cromwell's troops have left their camp (far right); some are still crossing the steep glen leading down to the sea. At the far left, the English cavalry meet the Scottish right wing, in a burst of gunfire; in the

centre left, pikemen of the two sides are in action; just above the glen the cavalry
of the Scottish left wing are routed and flee up the hill, leaving their devastated
camp

Dunnottar Castle, Grampian, was one of the few major strongholds left in Royalist
hands by the summer of 1651. As a result it was used for the safekeeping of precious
documents, money and the Scottish crown and sceptre. Parliamentarian forces laid siege
to it in the autumn of 1651, and the following summer the castle fell; the regalia,
however, were smuggled out to safety

Charles's aim – ever since that fatal day when he left Holland only
to learn on his way of the defeat of his most gallant and loyal Scots
follower, Montrose, cruelly hanged and quartered as a traitor – had
been to unite all his supporters in Scotland and England to fight
together for his restoration. The overthrow of the Covenanter army at
Dunbar gave Charles his opportunity, although it was not until
2 June 1651 that the Act of Classes which prevented the former
Engagers from serving in the army was repealed by the Scottish
Parliament. Meanwhile every effort had been exerted to revive the
flame of Royalism in England. The country was divided into districts

in which Royalist organizers began secret preparations. In Norfolk a premature rising had taken place before Christmas; a scheme was worked out for a landing at Dover Castle: in Lancashire Royalists were promised Scottish help if they could arouse the county's gentry, reputedly the most Royalist in England, on behalf of the King. The second Duke of Buckingham was provided with the nucleus of an army which it was hoped could be enlisted in the north-west and in North Wales. By this time many English Presbyterians were beginning to opt for monarchy. Had not Charles I offered to accept a Presbyterian Church while he was in the Isle of Wight? Had not the Presbyterian commanders like Essex and Manchester always been as loyal to the monarchy as to Parliament? A Presbyterian minister rejoicing in the name of Love was arrested in London during May for conspiring on behalf of the King. He and another minister were executed on Tower Hill at the beginning of August as a warning to all other Presbyterians actually sympathetic to Charles II.

Though the republican authorities throughout his southern kingdom were sufficiently watchful to prevent any serious risings unless and until Charles won a victory on English soil, in Scotland the King was at last supreme. He was accepted as nominal commander-in-chief of the Scottish army, while the sinister Marquis of Argyll, who had changed sides once too often, pleading his wife's illness retired in dudgeon to his Highland castle of Inverary. The winter put an end to hostilities. Leslie with the remains of his army, now gradually reinforced by Engagers and Royalist Highlanders, defied the English south of Stirling and along the line of the River Forth. Cromwell had made one or two attempts to outflank him both to the east and to the west of Stirling, but to no avail. The English commander-in-chief himself was taken ill in the course of an inclement winter and blustery spring, so that it was not until June that campaigning was vigorously resumed. On 17 July Colonel Robert Overton with a force of 1,600 men managed to cross the Forth by boats from South Queensferry to North Queensferry (where the old Forth Bridge was later to be built). Lambert then followed him across with a larger force and defeated a Scottish detachment which was sent to deal with him at the battle of Inverkeithing on 20 July. Thereupon Cromwell carried his whole army except for four cavalry and four infantry regiments across the river and made for

Used as the Royalists' base from September 1650, Stirling Castle was too strong to be threatened by a direct attack. It was eventually starved into surrender by George Monck

Perth, thus cutting the lines of communication of the Scots army. The Scots now had two alternatives if they were not to be surrounded – to fight where they stood or to march into England so as to sever Cromwell's own communications with the south. Understandably Charles II resolved on the latter alternative, which was approved by the leader of the Engagers, the second Duke of Hamilton, but not apparently by Leslie, who had so skilfully withstood Cromwell at Stirling. Charles hoped that, once in England, Royalists there would again rally to his side. That was why he chose the route through Carlisle, Warrington and Manchester where Royalism was still thought to be strong.

It has been said that the Scots army was less well trained and less

During the 1640s the Earl of Derby repulsed all opposition from parliamentary forces on the Isle of Man. Following Derby's capture and execution in 1651 all the Royalist strongholds fell, and the island was under Parliament's control for the remainder of the decade. The earthwork at Fort Loyal, built in 1648–9, is typical of civil war artillery works. The main artillery was located at the large arrowhead corner bastions, which were linked and surrounded by a bank, ditch and outer parapet

adequately armed than the English. It is not clear why this should have been so once all the Scots were permitted to serve the King, unless it was because the kingdom was poorer than England. But what is certain is that the hearts of many of the Scots who marched across the border – covering three hundred miles in three weeks – were not in the campaign; this was particularly true of Leslie who made gloomy prognostications *en route*. The size of this army is variously estimated: it may have been only just over 13,000 men. On the other hand, Cromwell's army had been reinforced since Dunbar, while Major-General Thomas Harrison commanded a cavalry force which had long been stationed near the border ready to repel invasion. The militiamen of the threatened northern counties were called up and Fleetwood had been sent south to collect a fresh army there. Cromwell tried to soothe fearful politicians in London by saying that they might have to suffer 'some inconveniences' but that his crossing of the Forth had been the only method of avoiding another year's campaign in Scotland.

Charles II's hopes of assistance from English Royalists – both Anglicans and Presbyterians – were dashed. The Earl of Derby had arrived from the Isle of Man to try to inspirit Lancashire, but Lancastrians had no reason to love the Scots. On 25 August Derby's small force was defeated at Wigan by a cavalry regiment under Colonel Robert Lilburne (brother of the Leveller leader, Freeborn John) and Derby himself fled to join the King. A Scottish general, the Earl of Middleton, was unsuccessful with recruiting in Wales. However Charles's army managed to brush aside a cavalry army commanded by Harrison and they also evaded Lambert, who had been sent ahead by Cromwell, and finally reached Worcester exhausted on 22 August. Charles was delighted to be greeted with a warm welcome from the Mayor, whom he knighted, and on Sunday 24 August was able to listen to an Anglican sermon preached in the cathedral. Yet few Midland Royalists came to his help, for they too were alienated by the Scots.

Cromwell had more than 28,000 men at his disposal when he caught up with Charles at Worcester. So he was able almost to surround the city. Fleetwood was put in command of a force which was instructed to ford the River Teme, a tributary of the Severn, and attack three fine Scottish regiments which were deployed south of the city. Cromwell placed his cannon to the east, intending, it seems, to attack the walled city simultaneously on two fronts. As at Dunbar, he assumed command of a reserve, consisting of his life-guards, his own regiment of horse, and three experienced infantry regiments, so that when Fleetwood was held up in crossing the Teme Oliver was able to relieve the pressure on his second-in-command by throwing a bridge of boats over the Severn, he himself leading his men across. Charles II, who could watch the operations

An Exact Ground-Plot of ye City of Worcester As it stood fortify'd, 3. Sept. 1651. The battle
was fought south and east of the city. The main attack went in across the rivers Teme
and Severn, but part of Cromwell's army with his artillery was posted on Red Hill to
the east of Fort Royal, where Charles II had his cannon. Charles watched the battle from
the cathedral tower. He ordered a counter-attack on Red Hill but was defeated on both
fronts

from the cathedral tower, tried to attack the Parliamentarian
artillery positions by a sortie uphill to the east of the city. The
struggle lasted three hours. Eventually the defenders of Worcester
were overwhelmed. Four thousand Scots who had taken little part in
the battle were pursued, cut off, and taken prisoner before they
could reach home. Oliver Cromwell described the victory as 'a
crowning mercy'. One of his chaplains, Hugh Peter, observed to the
English militia who had fought in the battle: 'When your wives and
children shall ask you where you have been, and what news: say you

Boscobel House, Shropshire. After the battle of Worcester Charles II lay in hiding here for two days, one of them spent in the famous oak tree

have been at Worcester, where England's sorrows began, and where they are happily ended.' For the first skirmish in the civil wars had been fought by Prince Rupert against Fiennes's men near Worcester almost precisely nine years earlier.

After Worcester another symbolic and romantic episode took place. Charles II himself, who had fought bravely until the very last, showing, it was said, 'much steadiness of mind and undaunted courage', succeeded after forty-five days of adventure, eluding every Roundhead soldier who would have liked to take him prisoner to reap a reward, in escaping across the sea to France. Almost everywhere he went he found loyal subjects to help him on his way. During these weeks he learned much about his countrymen and about their devotion to their religion, less ostentatious and less hypocritical, it

After a long exile on the continent, Charles II was persuaded to return to England by a mission to the Hague, led by Sir Thomas Fairfax in May 1660. Fairfax had become increasingly alienated from Cromwell and the Parliamentarian party over the years, firstly in his failure to condone the execution of Charles I and then with his refusal to lead an army into Scotland in 1650. Here Charles II is seen departing from Schveningen in Holland to regain the throne

seemed to him, than that of the overtly pious Scots. It was these ancient loyalties that in the end were to bring him back to his father's throne.

What were the consequences of these civil wars? If the events of 1641–2 constituted the eruption of the first English revolution, a second revolution had taken place in 1648 when the House of Commons was purged of those members who still wanted to come to an agreement with the King and to transform him into a constitu-

Engraved by H.Adlard from an original Painting in the Author's Possession.

(Fac-simile of his Signature and Seal to the Warrant for Beheading Charles I.st.)

Frontispiece to a publication of 1821, *Oliver Cromwell and His Times*: an engraving from an original painting and a facsimile of Cromwell's signature and seal on Charles I's death warrant

Detailed map of England, printed in 1668, showing the major cities, the fire of London, a list of the shires and their make up, and the dates of the English monarchs from William the Conqueror to Charles II

tional monarch. It is fascinating to contemplate what might have happened if the 'purged' members had had their way. For the remainder of his life Charles I might have been the same kind of figurehead that King Frederick I of Sweden was to be in the eighteenth century. A bigoted and exclusive Presbyterian Church, similar to the Scottish Kirk, might have been set up instead of the latitudinarian Anglican establishment which has endured until the present day. But what in fact happened was that Charles I was tried and executed, his son was comprehensively defeated in the third civil war, and two years later General Oliver Cromwell became Lord Protector of the Commonwealth.

Cromwell was not a dictator; he was required to accept the advice of his Council of State; moreover parliaments of one kind or another sat sporadically until the close of the Interregnum. Cromwell, however, was a strong man, a born leader, and a tolerant ruler. He allowed Jews to return to England; he permitted Roman Catholics and Anglicans to worship privately in London; and although he instituted a State Church with Triers and Ejectors instead of bishops and deans, he did not interfere with eccentric Christian sects so long as they behaved themselves. After his death anarchy broke loose. His son Richard was an ineffective Protector while the leading generals, Fleetwood, Lambert and Monck, quarrelled among themselves. So the realists throughout the country came to the conclusion that a return to monarchy was the only sure way to secure domestic peace.

The civil wars had three main constitutional results. The first was that the feudal rights of the Crown and the Tudor prerogative courts, which Charles I had agreed to abolish in 1641, were never to be restored. Secondly, the King's power to levy taxes (such as ship money) without the consent of the House of Commons or his right to arrest its members without showing cause was destroyed. Lastly, because Parliament won the civil wars it henceforward became an unchallengeable part of the British constitution. The Church of England ceased to be the sole religious institution because, in spite of heavy penalties imposed upon them, dissenters – known as nonconformists – emerged as a permanent feature of public life and influence on society.

Both Charles II and his brother, the future King James II, dreaded a renewal of the civil wars. Charles, an astute ruler, prevented the outbreak of civil war during the 'exclusionist crisis' of the 1670s when a majority in the Commons tried to prevent his Roman Catholic brother from succeeding to the throne. But James, though he became monarch without immediate opposition in 1685, provoked some of his leading subjects into rebellion and his own nephew and son-in-law, William of Orange, then invaded England with a powerful army and navy after receiving an invitation from them to do so. James lost his nerve and fled, first from his army headquarters at

Salisbury and then from his capital, rather than fight it out. So the Glorious Revolution of 1688 was a postscript to the Interregnum. Since then there have been no more civil wars in Great Britain.

ENGLANDS ROYAL PATTERN, or the History of K. CHARLES the FIRST, from his Marriage to his Death.

Bibliographical Note

In this note I confine myself chiefly to secondary authorities in book form because the original sources, ranging from contemporary reports to private letters and autobiographies, are difficult to select satisfactorily, while the articles in learned journals, notably the *Journal of the Society for Army Historical Research, The English Historical Review* and the *Bulletin of Historical Research*, are far too numerous to set out.

The standard volume covering all aspects of the time of the civil war is *Bibliography of British History: Stuart Period 1603–1714* (ed. Godfrey Davies and Mary Frear Keeler, 1970). A list of books and articles published since this volume appeared will be found in G.E. Aylmer, *Rebellion or Revolution?* (1986) and J.A.S. Morrill, *Seventeenth Century Britain* (1980).

For purely military history see the bibliographical essay in John Kenyon and the bibliography in Young and Holmes (IV below).

I. The Causes of the Civil War

This is a topic of continuing controversy among academic historians. Broadly these may be divided into those who stress long-term social and economic causes, e.g., Lawrence Stone, *The Causes of the English Revolution 1529–1642* (1973) and *The Crisis of the Aristocracy* (1965); the Marxists, e.g., Christopher Hill (ed.), *The English Revolution* (1955) and Brian Manning, *The English People and the English Revolution 1640–1649* (1976) and the more traditional political view originally expounded by S.R. Gardiner in his *History of the Great Civil War 1642–1649* (1893). See also in general Philip A.M. Taylor (ed.), *The Origins of the English Civil War: Conspiracy, Crusade or Class*

Conflict (1960); E.W. Innes (ed.), *The English Revolution 1600–1660* (1968); Conrad Russell (ed.), *The Origins of the English Civil War* (1973); F.D. Dow, *Radicalism in the English Revolution* (1985) and A. Fletcher, *The Outbreak of the English Civil War* (1981).

II. General History

Four excellent recent summaries covering the civil war period are B. Coward, *The Stuart Age 1603–1714* (1980); Derek Hirst, *Authority and Conflict 1603–1714* (1985); J.S. Morrill, *Seventeenth Century Britain 1603–1714* (1980); Ivan Roots, *The Great Rebellion 1642–1660* (1979). For a fine, purely narrative history see C.V. Wedgwood, *The King's War 1641–1647* (1958).

III. County Histories

Events in most English counties during the civil war have received detailed study. These include E.A. Andriette, *Devon and Exeter in the Civil War* (1971); A.R. Bayley, *The Great Civil War in Dorset* (1961); E. Broxap, *The Great Civil War in Lancashire 1642–1651* (1910); J.T. Cliffe, *Yorkshire Gentry* (1969); Mary Coate, *Cornwall in the Great Civil War and Interregnum 1642–1660* (1963); R.N. Dore, *The Civil War in Cheshire* (1968); A.M. Everitt, *The County Committee of Kent in the Civil War* (1957), (ed.) *Suffolk and the Great Rebellion 1640–1660* (1960) and *The Community of Kent and the Great Rebellion* (1966); W.G. Farrow, *The Civil War in Shropshire* (1926); A. Fletcher, *A County Community in Peace and War: Sussex 1600–1660* (1976); G.N. Godwin, *The Civil War in Hampshire* (1904); R. Howell, *Newcastle upon Tyne and the Puritan Revolution* (1967); Ann Hughes, *Politics, Society and Civil War in Warwickshire* (1987); R.W. Ketton-Kremer, *Norfolk in the Civil War* (1969); A. Kingston, *Hertfordshire in the Great Civil War* (1894); J.S. Morrill, *Cheshire 1630–1660* (1974); Valerie Pearl, *London on the Outbreak of the Puritan Revolution* (1961); D.H. Pennington and Ivan Roots, *The Committee at Stafford 1643–1645* (1957); R.N. Reckitt, *Charles the First and Hull* (1952); David Underdown, *Somerset in the Civil War and Interregnum* (1973); F.J. Varley, *The Siege of Oxford: Oxford during the Civil War 1642–1646* (1932); J. Willis-Bund, *The Civil War in Worcestershire* (1905); A.C. Wood, *Nottinghamshire in the*

Civil War (1934). C. Holmes, *The Eastern Association in the English Civil War* (1974) and R.E. Sherwood, *Civil War in the Midlands* (1974) are also important.

IV. Military History

For the general background see in particular Michael Roberts, 'The Military Revolution 1560–1660' in *Essays in Swedish History* (1967) and Geoffrey Parker, *The Military Revolution: Military innovation and the rise of the West 1500–1800* (1988).

For biographies of generals see John Adair, *Roundhead General: a Military Biography of Sir William Waller* (1969); Maurice Ashley, *Prince Rupert of the Rhine* (1976) and *Cromwell's Generals* (1954); F.T.R. Edgar, *Sir Ralph Hopton* (1968); Clements Markham, *Great Lord Fairfax* (1870); Vernon F. Snow, *Essex the Rebel* (1970).

For the battles: John Adair, *Cheriton* (1975); Barry Denton, *Naseby Fight* (1985); Peter Newman, *The Battle of Marston Moor* (1981); Margaret Toynbee and Peter Young, *Cropredy Bridge 1644* (1970); Peter Young, *Edgehill 1642* (1947), *Marston Moor 1644* (1967), *Naseby 1645* (1985).

For the armies: C.H. Firth, *Cromwell's Army* (1962); C.H. Firth and Godfrey Davies, *The Regimental History of Cromwell's Army* (1940); Ronald Hutton, *The Royalist War Effort 1642–1646* (1982); Peter Young and Wilfrid Emberton, *The Cavalier Army* (1974).

General books on the civil war covering military history include Austin Woolrych, *Battles of the Civil War* (1954); Peter Young and Richard Holmes, *The English Civil War* (1974) and John Kenyon, *The Civil Wars in England* (1985). For the navy there is J.R. Powell, *The Navy in the English Civil War* (1962).

Index

Illustrations and maps are shown in italic.

Maurice, Prince, 76, 80, 90
Merchants, 3, 16, 61
Militia, control of, 96, 97
Militia, the London, 65, 73
Molyneux, Lord, 107
Monck, George, Colonel, 95, *103*, 179, 192
Montagu, Edward, Lord Mandeville later 2nd Earl of Manchester, 54, 90, 95, 105, 110, 115 *seq.*, 120 *seq.*; character, 121
Montrose, 1st Marquis of, *see* Graham, James

Naseby, battle of, 64, 67, 127 *seq.*, *130*, 135
Newark, 78, 94, 102, 120, 136, 138, *140*, *141*
Newbury, 82; 1st battle of, 82 *seq.*, *84*, 86, 88; 2nd battle of, 116 *seq.*, *117*, 120, 121
Newcastle upon Tyne, 16, 63, 112–13, *113*, 114, 119, 123, 138, 145
Newcastle, Duke of, *see* Cavendish, William
New Model Army, 123 *seq.*, 137, 138, 145, 148, 149, 155
Nineteen propositions, the, 57
Norfolk, 8, 182
Northampton, 66
Northamptonshire, 139
Northumberland, 40, 94
Nottingham, 59, 66, 138
Nottinghamshire, 94
Nye, Philip, 90

Okey, John, Colonel, 127, 129
Ormonde, Marquis of, *see* Butler, James
Oxford, 72, 73, 75, 78, 85, 88, 97

seq., 115, 118, 125, *135*, *138*, 141–2, 143; siege, 125; surrender, 138

Parliament, the Short, 39, 41
Parliament, the Long, 40
Penington, Isaac, 54
Petition of Right, the, 24, 28
Philiphaugh, battle of, 136
Plymouth, *110*, 113, 119
Pontefract, 158, 159
Portsmouth, 55, 114
Presbyterianism, 14, 31, 35, 119, 123, 138, 145, 150, 166, 183, 191
Preston, battle of, 87, 159 *seq.*, 172
Privy Council, the, 45
Puritans, the, *11*, 12, 13, 14, 18, 30, 31, 152
Pym, John, 14, 21, 23, 24, 28, 30, 39, 41, 42 *seq.*, *42*, 54, 55, 63, 73, 78, 82, 88

Rich, Robert, 2nd Earl of Warwick, 39, 67
Roman Catholics, 21, 31, 56, 132, 192
Rupert, Prince of the Palatinate, 63, 67 *seq.*, 80 *seq.*, 94, 96 *seq.*, 105, 106 *seq.*, 117, 125 *seq.*, 135 *seq.*, 155
Ruthven, Patrick, Lord Forth and Earl of Brentford, 63, 99, 117

St John Oliver, 46
Salisbury, 116
Scotland, 1, 33, 35 *seq.*, 51, 53, 82, 90, 125, 174 *seq.*
Self-Denying Ordinance, 123
Seymour, Edward, 2nd Earl and

Marquis of Worcester, 6, 61,
136
Shaw House, 117, 121
Ship money, 10–11, 35, 48
Shrewsbury, 66
Skippon, Philip, Major-General,
84–5, 128, 129, 147
Solemn League and Covenant, 88,
88, 89
Somerset, 30, 61
Spain, 2, 21, 24
Speen village, 116–17
Stirling, 184, *184*
Strafford, Earl of, *see* Wentworth,
Sir Thomas
Suffolk, 8, 143

Taunton, 113, 124, 125, 134
Tonnage and poundage, 8–9, 24,
26, 31, 48

Ulster, 51, 172

Vane, Sir Henry the Younger, 39,
41, 44, 61, 82, 88, 99
Verney, Sir Edmund, 42, 61, 72
Villiers, George, 1st Duke of
Buckingham, 21, *22*, *23*, 24,
25, 28, 30, 32, 53

Wales, 8, 80, 134, 135, 186
Walker, Sir Edward, quoted,
129–30
Waller, Sir William, Major-
General, 61, *62*, 76, 80, 82,
90, 94, 97 *seq.*, *107*, 114, 116,
123; quoted, 116
Warwick, 2nd Earl of, *see* Rich,
Robert
Warwick Castle, *65*
Watson, Lionel, Scoutmaster-
General, quoted, 107, 109, 110
Wentworth, Sir Thomas, Viscount
and Earl of Strafford, 33, *34*, 37
seq., 42 *seq.*, *46*, 51
Whitehall palace, 47, 54
Whitelocke, Bulstrode, 41
Wiltshire, 80, 138
Windsor Castle, 72, 78, 124
Worcester, 66, 186, *187*, 188;
battle of, 186 *seq.*
Worcester, Earl of, *see* Seymour,
Edward

Yeomen, 3, 6, 16, 142
York, 56, 94, 99 *seq.*, 119
Yorkshire, 30, 61, 75, 76, 77, 78,
95, 114, 128